PICTURING ILLINOIS

Picturing
ILLINOIS

Twentieth-Century Postcard Art from Chicago to Cairo

JOHN A. JAKLE
AND KEITH A. SCULLE

University of Illinois Press
Urbana, Chicago, and Springfield

Library of Congress Cataloging-in-Publication Data
Jakle, John A.
Picturing Illinois : twentieth-century postcard art from
Chicago to Cairo / John A. Jakle and Keith A. Sculle.
p.   cm.
Includes bibliographical references and index.
ISBN 978-0-252-03682-8
1. Postcards—Illinois—History—20th century.
2. Illinois—History—20th century—Pictorial works.
3. Chicago (Ill.)—History—20th century—Pictorial works.
4. City and town life—Illinois—History—20th century—
Pictorial works.
5. Country life—Illinois—History—20th century—
Pictorial works.
 I. Sculle, Keith A. II. Title.
F542.J35   2012
977.30022'2—dc23   2012022890

For Cindy and Tracey

CONTENTS

PREFACE AND ACKNOWLEDGMENTS

Some one hundred years ago, the lowly postcard prompted a true enthusiasm for popular visual art. Scenic postcards were mailed and collected annually quite literally by the hundreds of millions, thus coming to play a vital role in how Americans conceptualized their nation's geography. Through postcard art, Americans learned what was important both in big cities such as Chicago and in small-town and rural locales beyond. Postcards pictured the important aspects of local landscapes and places, especially buildings, streets, and parks. They taught how such things were best visualized. So also did they help to anchor Americans in history. As often as not, what got pictured spoke to a sense of progress over time whereby life in the United States had only gotten better, at least in regard to things material. For many Americans, the consumption of postcard art became a form of self-congratulation. Postcards said: "I belong here." "This is my place." "This is my kind of place."

Well before 1900, when postcards' popularity soared, Chicagoans had already come to think of their city, and by extension themselves, as something largely apart from the remainder of the state of Illinois—almost a state in its own right. And for good reason: Chicago had become the economic capital of a vast Middle Western region that stretched from the High Plains and the Rocky

Mountains in the west to the Appalachians in the east, and from the Canadian border southward to the Ohio River and the Ozark Uplands.

A word about nomenclature is in order at the outset. Today, Illinoisans colloquially refer to Chicago as including Cook County, and to locales beyond as "Downstate," including the remainder of northern Illinois. Excepted, of course, are the so-called collar counties, which contain Chicago's outer suburbs and which, accordingly, are also very much part of the Chicago metropolis. For occasional convenience, "Downstate" and "downstaters" are used throughout this book, but for certainty that two domains exist in Illinois and in recognition of Chicago's elite cultural and economic supremacy beyond the state boundaries, the term "beyond the metropolis" is applied often throughout the text. For its part, Downstate Illinois was quintessentially Middle Western, comprising a mix of small cities (albeit molded in Chicago's image), small towns, farms, and wilder landscapes and spaces.

The dichotomy between Chicago and Illinois beyond the metropolis was, of course, a false one. Chicago's wealth depended upon its central location within an emergent regional transportation infrastructure: lake and river shipping, shipping by canal (the Illinois and Michigan Canal most importantly), the moving of people and freight by railroad, then by automobile and motor truck, and finally by air. Thus it was that the resources of a broad hinterland moved to Chicago's factories and workshops, including corn, wheat, cattle, hogs, lumber, cotton, coal, and petroleum. Flowing back the other way were industrial products, such as iron and steel, finished lumber and millwork, and farm implements, as well as a growing array of consumer goods from wholesalers and retailers, including mail-order houses. Chicago was also the Middle West's premier financial center. But without its supportive hinterland, with its rich soils and abundance of industrial raw materials and its consuming population, there could not have been a Chicago. Chicago and Downstate Illinois existed in necessary symbiosis. In this book, we examine that symbiosis by looking at how Chicagoans and downstaters saw their geography visually depicted through postcard art a century ago.

In the early twentieth century, Chicago was America's boom metropolis, the pride not just of its citizens but of Illinoisans in general, and of midwesterners and, for that matter, most Americans as well. What the United States was thought to be, both at its very best and at its very worst, seems to have been symbolized there. No assessment of the American experience was complete without somehow "picturing" life as lived in Chicago, but, as we would emphasize, neither was it complete without considering life as lived in the city's Middle Western hinterland. From beyond the metropolis had come Abraham Lincoln, the martyred savior of the nation. Without Lincoln, the American political order, so essential to the nation's economic progress, might not have survived the Civil War. The whole state of Illinois begged to be pictured, especially in postcard art.

No other American city, save perhaps New York City, attracted more attention from postcard publishers than Chicago. Indeed, given its central location and its status as a major printing and publishing center, the city became a leading producer and distributor of postcards nationwide. Chicago was North America's principal railroad hub and, accordingly, the nation's leading convention site. The hosting of the 1893 World's Columbian Exposition launched the city as a major tourist attraction. In a mere sixty years, Chicago had grown to become the world's fourth-largest metropolis, a feat accomplished despite the setback of the city's destructive 1871 fire. Early-twentieth-century boosters predicted that Chicago would surely become the entire nation's economic capital.

The city was spoken of in superlatives. In the words of the poet Carl Sandburg, Chicago was

Hog Butcher for the World
Tool Maker, Stacker of Wheat
Player with Railroads and the Nation's
    Freight Handler,
Stormy, husky, brawling,
City of the Big Shoulders.

"I should like to go to America, if only to see that Chicago," said Chancellor Otto von Bismarck, founder of the modern German state. The British actress Sarah Bernhardt did visit the city: "I adore Chicago," she exclaimed. "It is the pulse of America."

As souvenirs, postcards provided visitors as well as residents with a visual record of what might be (and, more importantly, what ought to be) seen and done in a given place. The postcards that were sent to friends and relatives constituted proof of place experience. For those who could not travel, postcards supplied a kind of visual knowing: a means of vicarious comprehension through armchair perusal. As postcards suggested what was important to see, so also did they suggest how those things should be visualized. View cards did more than just depict; ever so subtly, they implied what viewers ought to believe about a place. Taken in sum, the cards of any locality sought to persuade, if not by what they showed, then by what they did not show.

Illinois beyond the metropolis benefited from Chicago's prominence as a tourist attraction. In order to reach Chicago, travelers had to make their way across the rest of the state. However, with the fiftieth anniversary of Abraham Lincoln's death in 1915, Downstate Illinois, especially Springfield, became a destination in its own right, as travelers made pilgrimages to the "Land of Lincoln." Downstate also offered a contrast with Chicago. Images of farming, small-town life, and small-city life could be variously interpreted against the shadow of the great metropolis. Life downstate

was viewed as simpler, less hurried, and perhaps even more American, in that it was less affected by perceived big-city problems, including rapidly increasing foreign immigration, emasculation of skilled labor through mechanization, and growing social inequality and political disfranchisement, as well as persisting crime and increasing environmental degradation.

People comprehend the world in terms of places: centers of attention that nest in landscape as meaningful settings for behavior. Places function and are interlinked at various geographical scales in facilitating human socialization. In visualizing landscape, the meaning of one's surroundings is interpreted on the basis of one's intentionality at the moment. Sought is some kind of comforting predictability that establishes the familiar, an imagined geography that can enhance life's satisfactions while diminishing its dissatisfactions. Who people consider themselves to be hinges substantially on how they see themselves positioned geographically in the world. By 1900, postcard views had become especially important in framing and communicating the meaning of place. Postcards enhanced people's understanding of places, thus helping to establish place expectations in everyday life as well as in travel. "Few graphic novelties have achieved so rich and evocative a history," observed historian Neil Harris. Postcards, he wrote, were simultaneously "instruments of communication, statements of identity, and records of activity." Through postcard views, viewers could readily insert themselves mentally into places.

Scholars have tended to disparage postcard art for its conventionality. Priced at but a few cents apiece, postcards were marketed to a broad and largely uncritical popular audience. Narrow profit margins tended to preclude artistic innovation. Thus compositional and other formulas were repeated over and over again to produce a kind of "pop art" with mass appeal. However, it was through that uniformity and standardization that postcards came to exert a profound influence on what Americans thought about their geography. Certain kinds of views, when encountered over and over again, spoke with a sort of authority: a sense of truthfulness emerging through an apparent stamp of public acceptance. In adopting conventional subjects and compositional rules, postcard publishers inadvertently simplified the complexity of the American scene, making places familiar in easily anticipated ways. True, postcards needed to tell comforting stories in a straightforward way. Accordingly, they rarely depicted the unsavory. Nonetheless, implicit in their conventionality were cultural values, and indeed ideological stances, many of which we sustain today.

Through vintage postcard art, one can see not just what the past looked like but also what people were once encouraged to see and think about the time in which they were living. But more than mere intellectualization is to be had. Postcard images can be viewed metaphorically both as windows and as mirrors. They enable us to enter a past scene to look around, but they also invite us, having done so, to assess ourselves in reflection. What was it like back then? Why was it so? But also: How does it compare with what we see today? What lessons might we learn and apply?

Postcards extended the gaze of the nineteenth-century Parisian flâneur. As outlined by the philosopher Walter Benjamin, the flâneur walked the streets of Paris with no other purpose than to observe life. Flâneurs included journalists and other writers whose essays celebrated their ability to candidly situate themselves within the swirl of Parisian street life. They sought to impose order on the potentially disorienting diversity of the city by "reducing it to accessible images that could be collected and consumed." Flâneurs embraced not just spectacle or the spectacular but also life's subtleties, comprehension that required sensitive "envisioning." When postcard views became available, they enabled everyone to play the flâneur's game. For travelers, buying and sending postcards negated their having to record for themselves what they had observed. Purchased views made it possible for the armchair travelers back home to see the same sights, if only vicariously.

Postcards provided images around which travel itineraries could be set. They helped form travel expectations, and, more importantly, they provided mental constructs against which those expectations could be validated (or invalidated). When postcards were sent to others, they established the traveler's status as a spender of leisure time, and as an observer of important things. Of course, postcards could be used to send brief messages quite apart from travel. Previously, "postal cards," which carried a preprinted message and originally could be printed only by the U.S. Postal Service, were widely used in business, especially for advertising. But it was primarily because of tourism that the postcard, especially the view card, rapidly achieved widespread popularity. It was mainly through travel-related postcard art that landscape-oriented photography came before the eyes of ordinary Americans.

What view cards actually depicted of a given locality was, of course, determined by the postcard makers. As postcard photographers were directed to scenes thought to be of interest to tourists, or for that matter of interest to a locality's residents, places were symbolically reconstructed from selected points of view, and even from a limited range of actual viewpoints. Such orientation was fraught with social meaning. Today a social theorist might refer to "regimes of visual meaning" or to "discursive formations" in intellectually assigning the strategies by which symbolic values were imaginatively extracted from landscape and place and communicated photographically.

At base was a kind of "mindscaping": the reifying of specific features of landscape and of place as image sets supportive of selected social, economic, and political agendas. Landscapes depicted in postcard art were meant to convey specific messages and moods by picturing icons of place. Indeed, that iconography helped shape what places actually became.

In an introductory essay, we outline the principal historical and geographical themes by which vintage postcard images of Chicago and Downstate Illinois might be interpreted. We also treat the rise of postcard publishing in Chicago, the bulk of the Midwest's postcard art having originated there. Two essays follow, one devoted to Chicago and the other to Illinois beyond the metropolis, in which specific postcard views are interpreted for content and meaning, especially from the points of view of travelers, journalists, and others—observations about landscape and place made by writers of the period. Discovering meaning is a process of intertextual analysis. Landscape itself might be thought of as a kind of text waiting to be read: a kind of discourse to be interpreted. So also might representations of landscape—such as postcard views—be considered as such. But it is mainly through the use of words that people do their conceptualizing and their remembering. It is through words that people most effectively communicate with one another. In this regard, we pay close attention to the captions printed on the postcards, as well as the personal messages written on cards that were mailed. Information on each postcard's provenance is given in the credits.

The images reproduced herein date from 1893, the year of the World's Columbian Exposition, through 1965. The very few images included from the 1950s and 1960s are intended to offer a contrast with those of earlier decades, in regard both to changing photographic and printing tech-niques and, more importantly, to changing geographical themes. The majority of the views date to between 1900 and 1920, the so-called "golden age" of the postcard, when quality halftone printing came to the fore and postcards were at their height as a faddish novelty. There are also numerous cards from the 1930s, when highly colorful but heavily retouched views on "linen" paper (so called because of the texture created by its high rag content) were marketed in an attempt to revive sagging postcard sales. Photochromes (a form of color lithograph), cheaper to produce but less engaging visually, came to dominate after World War II.

Most color postcards were made by large commercial publishing houses, and were thus intended for mass marketing. We also include black-and-white "real photo postcard" views more characteristic of the Middle West's small-town photography studios, issued mainly for limited-market distribution. As well do we include black-and-white views made by amateur photographers solely for their own use. Eastman Kodak, among other companies, made available developing and printing equipment, as well as postcard-sized printing papers, to encourage home production of postcard art. These may be the cards that offer the most intimate understandings as to how people once valued not just landscapes and places but themselves.

[ ]

The fruition of a project such as this book from a personal vision shared intensely over a long period requires the support of many. Thanks are due especially to Willis G. Regier, Director, University of Illinois Press; the staff of the press; copyeditor Jane Lyle; and the anonymous reviewers. The staffs of the Abraham Lincoln Presidential Library and the Illinois State Library made research possible in often rare sources.

PICTURING ILLINOIS

INTRODUCTION

If Chicago was the great American success story, how could the city and its state possibly escape the focus of postcard representation? From a frontier trading post, Chicago had risen seemingly overnight to become one of the world's largest metropolises. As the twentieth century dawned, Illinois was both the nation's leading agricultural state and its third-leading industrial state. It was part of the prosperous Middle Western heartland, perhaps the most quintessentially American of regions. Around 1900, when the picture postcard craze hit the United States, Chicago and Illinois beyond the metropolis offered scenes variously spectacular, picturesque, and fundamentally American. Indeed, the picturing of Illinois not only fostered a substantial catalog of postcard art, but made Chicago an important production and distribution center for a booming postcard industry.

Chicago was certainly Mid-America's main postcard attraction. But fully appreciating what Chicago had become required an understanding of its surroundings—its regional context—and not just the city itself. Chicago influenced, and was influenced by, an extensive hinterland of small cities, small towns, and rural countryside. Like all big cities, it was knit into larger fabrics: real worlds of people and things fully contained by landscape, as well as imagined worlds of belief and attitude centered in people's minds. The images produced in the past enable us to explore those worlds today. Vintage postcards make it possible for us to see what they saw, and, equally important, to understand what it was that they were encouraged to visualize. "How do I hold you, city, in the mind / When my backward memory goes exploring?" So asked Christopher Morley in the opening lines of his poem "Chicago."

THE PAST IN POSTCARD ART

Picture postcards readily sustain an objectivist view of history, supplying facts as to what existed when and where. One can look at a card and make a judgment about what did or did not exist in a place as pictured. But we see postcard scenes as both inside and outside the flux of time. We also subscribe to what has come to be termed the constructionist view of history, in which the past continues to reside with those in the present who look back in time and assign meaning to what it is they think they see. Picture postcards are historical documents whose contents their creators negotiated with a former audience, a postcard-buying public. Consequently, they can yield meaningful insights about not just what, but how people in the past imagined places such as Chicago and Downstate Illinois to have been. Why were certain views selected? Why were they pictured as they were? What did it all mean? Equally as important, what might (even what ought) it mean to us today?

Viewers of Illinois postcards early in the twentieth century were intended to see mainly the positive. Put before them were images that spoke in superlatives: of technical prowess, of economic prosperity, and, as well, of the cultural accouterments of heightened civility that seemingly derived therefrom. Views of State Street, Chicago's main retail street, were highly favored, especially those that featured one or another of the city's large department stores. An advertising postcard circulated by Chicago's Yellow Cab Company

(FIGURE 1) shows the clock at Marshall Field's at the corner of State and Madison Streets. The intersection is swarming with the company's taxis. Like all early multicolored postcards, this image started out in black and white, with overlays of colored ink added in the printing process. Here a yellow hue clearly dominates. With such depictions, postcard viewers were invited to see places as delighted visitors would see them: to witness, thereby, the successes of modern life, life now fully removed from the primitiveness, if not the savagery, of what had only a short time before been a wilderness frontier. Although wilder images of nature (where nature appeared to be unspoiled) and pastoral images of farm life (where nature appeared improved through human stewardship) could readily be purchased as postcard views, the bulk of Illinois's postcard art celebrated urban places, especially Chicago. Indeed, the state's smaller cities, and even its small towns, were often pictured as if they were very much like Chicago: wannabe places seemingly as urbane as the big metropolis itself.

Photographers traditionally emphasized the grand and the monumental in picturing urban places. That was what sold, especially to more affluent customers, who largely preferred to ignore, and often denied, the unseemly aspects of life. Historian Peter Hales described how nineteenth-century depictions of impressive city scenes created a template for people to use in thinking about their own lives: "By plucking buildings out of their immediate surroundings and revealing them, within the picture's frame, in their grandest and most awesome perspective, these photographs served to celebrate the city's monumental symbols and to promulgate the composite mythos of prosperity and permanence," he wrote.

Historian Alison Isenberg similarly assessed the values underlying twentieth-century postcard views of downtown business districts, in

FIGURE 1. State Street, Chicago, 1925.

both large-sized and medium-sized cities nationwide. Postcard publishers liberally improved street scenes through dubbing: changing the appearance of things through both omission and addition. For example, they removed what many planners labeled the "pole and wire evil": the arrays of vertical poles between which telephone and power lines stretched often in visual chaos, in opposition to evolving modernism's sense of order and functionality. They also dubbed in automobiles and motor trucks where none actually existed, thus updating places and making them seem more progressive. Favored were "corridor perspectives," in which building facades of similar height were depicted from an angle that made them appear uninterrupted, the eye grandly carried off toward an implied vanishing point. Such picturing celebrated not what business districts were actually like so much as what they ought to

have been like. Isenberg, like Hales, invites us to think in terms of idealized landscapes and places when viewing postcard art.

Strong social assertion underlay such idealization. Landscape views privileged society's elites, especially its business class. The business of the United States was business, or so the popular saying went. Thus views of commercial districts became preeminent in the postcard publisher's representation of cities. It was the businessman's community that was celebrated, a community invariably dominated by white males who were variously networked through their commercial dealings and their social clubs, as well as through church membership. Race, class, and gender—the major fault lines in the apparently placid world of commerce—seldom entered the postcard pictorial record. Women in these images were relegated mainly to parks or shopping streets; they were seldom pictured at work, or in pursuit of occupations beyond the home. Rarely was the conflict between labor and management depicted. All the wrenching dislocations of a society in rapid transition from agriculture to industry—from farm and small-town life to metropolitan living—tended to be ignored.

To sell, postcards needed to set a reassuring tone. They needed to celebrate and not criticize. Buyers wanted reassurance. They wanted to feel, if only through the card's purchase, that they fit comfortably into the pictured scenes: that they indeed shared in America's successes. Consequently, postcards tended to leave the status quo largely unchallenged. Of course, there was always much in that status quo to be celebrated. Despite the many unresolved problems, Illinois's, and especially Chicago's, rapid rise was impressive by whatever measure. The quick growth of Chicago, the entire state, and indeed the entire Middle West was an unprecedented achievement in human history. What had happened in and around Chicago was the envy of the world. Perhaps, in keeping with the tenor of the times, the early publishers of postcards depicting Chicago and Illinois beyond the metropolis might be forgiven their celebratory stance?

In 1910, more than 2.1 million people lived in Chicago, about seven times the number of only sixty years before. The city was second in size in the United States, and fourth in the world. In 1910, Chicago ranked first in the nation in meat-packing, farm implement manufacture, and steel-making capacity, and second in printing and publishing. Seventy-eight percent of the population was foreign-born or had parents who were foreign-born, making the city one of the most cosmopolitan places in the world, at least in terms of cultural mix. African Americans, however, were few, making up less than 2 percent of the state's entire population. Statewide, there lived some 5.6 million people, most of them in urban places (nearly 62 percent) rather than rural areas (just over 38 percent), the balance between urban and rural living having tilted with the 1890 census. Average population density statewide stood at 100.6 persons per square mile, up from 45.4 only forty years earlier. The state ranked third in the nation in population size, with more inhabitants than all but a few of the world's nations at the time.

Some 211 miles across at its broadest and 381 miles long, Illinois encompassed some 56,665 square miles, an area as large as the United Kingdom. Its rivers, especially the Mississippi, the Ohio, and the Illinois, had readily opened up the state to both settlement and trade. Fresh water was abundant everywhere, from surface streams as well as from seasonal precipitation and underground aquifers. The state's relatively flat terrain was amenable not just to farming but to railroad and later modern highway construction. In 1910, twenty railroad lines radiated out across Illinois from Chicago and fifteen from St. Louis, with another dozen or so crossing the state from north to south or from east to west in avoidance of those cities. Railroads, in other words, formed a dense transportation infrastructure upon which the state's lesser cities and towns grew. The state's soils, especially those derived from glacial deposition and covered for millennia by prairie grasses, were unexcelled for agriculture, at least once they were drained. With more than 10.5 million acres planted in corn by 1905, Illinois competed annually with Iowa to be first in corn production. Soft coal underlay approximately two-thirds of the state, Illinois ranking second in its production. And the state was the nation's third-largest producer of crude oil. Such statistics were certainly impressive. Boosters could glory in them.

The popular sense of history that most Americans embraced early in the twentieth century involved prideful celebration. They had a largely uncritical view of what mainstream America had accomplished. The nation was celebrated as a land of opportunity: a place of unbridled progress where the democratic embrace of political liberty—supportive of a largely laissez-faire capitalism—rapidly encouraged economic growth and development. To many Americans, the nation's good fortunes appeared divinely inspired, although successes—at least personal successes—might also be ascribed to intelligence, hard work, and even just plain good luck. There was little in the nation's postcard art to suggest otherwise. Postcard publishers did their best to reinforce the typical American's sense of pride. Americans deserved to glory in the fruits of their labors. Postcard buyers embraced images that positively reinforced what most Americans believed the United States to be. Indeed, the nation's postcard craze was largely a matter of self-congratulation.

HISTORY AS CHANGING GEOGRAPHY

Native Americans first settled the area that became Illinois. The Cahokians were perhaps the most significant in prehistory, given that around 700 A.D. they built a huge mound complex across the Mississippi River from present-day St. Louis, an urban-like ceremonial place with a population of more than 10,000. A portion of the huge Monk's Mound (so called because French monks once operated a monastery on its crown) still survives near Collinsville. A millennium later, when the French arrived, Native Americans were hardly thriving in the area, their numbers having been greatly decimated, first by the spread of disease and then by intertribal warfare, both of which had been precipitated by European contacts far to the south and east. In 1673, Louis Joliet and Father Jacques Marquette, having explored the lower Mississippi River, turned up the Illinois River toward Canada, coming upon a village of the Kaskaskia near present-day Ottawa. French

explorers, missionaries, and traders came to refer to that group, and to the other small Indian bands affiliated with them, as the "Illinois." Hence the name of the river, and also of the state.

"Les Pays des Illinois" was strategically located at midcontinent. To the north, by way of the Des Plaines and Chicago Rivers, was a short portage to Lake Michigan. By another portage, connecting Lake Huron and Georgian Bay with the Ottawa River, access could be had to the St. Lawrence River, and ultimately to the Atlantic beyond. To the south, by way of the Illinois River, the Lower Mississippi River offered direct access to the Gulf of Mexico. Beginning in the 1690s, French colonial settlement centered around several small trading villages downstream from today's St. Louis, including Cahokia, Prairie du Rocher, and Kaskaskia in Illinois and Ste. Genevieve in Missouri. The east bank of the Mississippi came under the control of Britain following the French and Indian War, and under the control of Virginia and the new United States following the American Revolution. Kaskaskia became the territorial capital of a new Illinois Territory in 1809, and the capital of the new state of Illinois in 1818.

By 1900, little that was tangible of the French occupation remained. What did remain was treated very much as a curiosity, for example, the eighteenth-century French habitant's house at Cahokia that early in the nineteenth century had served as St. Clair County's first courthouse (**FIGURE 2**). Displayed at the World's Columbian Exposition in 1893, it languished in Chicago's Jackson Park as an authentic reminder not only of a time lost, but of the state's (and Chicago's) rapid development thereafter. The handwritten message on the reverse side of this postcard reads: "We went to Jackson Park and ate dinner on the porch of this building [which was] under three flags—that means stars and stripes, the English Union Jack, and the French Tri-color" (actually the yellow fleur-de-lis).

Jackson Park, Chicago,
Cohokia Court House, Wooded Island.
The Oldest Court House in the State of Illinois.

FIGURE 2. Cahokia Courthouse, Jackson Park, Chicago, ca. 1905.

The pioneer era followed, as settlers flooded into Illinois. During the nascent phase of the market economy in the state, transportation principally combined manpower and animal power (mainly horses and oxen) with primitive steam engines, but also relied heavily on water currents. Early on, flatboats carried Illinois's farm surpluses down the various rivers to New Orleans. After 1820, steamboats routinely plied the Ohio and the Mississippi, as well as the Great Lakes, making cities such as Cincinnati, and especially Buffalo, with its Erie Canal connection to New York City, principal markets for Illinois produce. It was the Illinois and Michigan Canal, however, that truly energized Chicago and made it a metropolis. With the canal's completion in 1848, grain collected from the state's central interior could be sent east via Chicago and the Great Lakes, not only cheaply, but relatively quickly.

Railroading developed slowly in Illinois, initially to help funnel agricultural and other commodities to the port of Chicago. The city's earliest railroads radiated outward from the city toward the west and northwest to tap the trade of the Upper Mississippi Valley, thereby diverting that trade from St. Louis. The 1850s saw the completion of the Illinois Central Railroad, a 700-mile line (the world's longest at the time) between Cairo on the south and Galena on the north; the project was subsidized through a large federal land grant, the first of its kind. A branch line northeastward from Centralia to Chicago became the Illinois Central's actual mainline, the railroad later calling itself the "Mainline of Mid-America." The rise of commercial agriculture energized the towns, particularly the thousands of new towns that grew up at regular intervals along the new railroads.

Rush St. Bridge, Across Chicago River, Chicago.

FIGURE 3. The Chicago River at Rush Street, ca. 1905.

Of course, Chicago attracted much of the region's industrial activity, also becoming its financial center, largely in partnership with New York City and Boston capitalists. Eastern money flowed in to fund industry and commerce, to build the railroads, and to drive a real estate boom through construction of the city itself. Chicago quickly became the world's largest railroad center, as well as its premier grain trading and handling center, lumber distributor, stockyard center, farm implement manufacturer, railroad car maker, and iron and steel producer. The railroads, like the Illinois and Michigan Canal before, carried wheat and corn by the carload to giant grain elevators built along the Chicago River (FIGURE 3). Negated was the shipping of grain in barrels or in sacks—the handling of grain, in other words, as finite assets belonging to specific owners. Once graded, the

grain was mixed as a generic commodity to be sold in bulk through the city's Board of Trade.

In the lumber trade, Chicago merchants were positioned between the source of timber in Michigan and Wisconsin and lumber retailers spread across the United States, but especially westward to the Rocky Mountains and beyond. Pork and beef slaughter and the processing of meat brought international acclaim to the city, both for the giant scale of the industry and for its assembly-line (or dis-assembly-line) methods. No visit to Chicago was deemed complete without a visit to the city's killing and packing floors. The production of farm implements furthered the city's rise, as did the manufacture of railroad equipment. Chicago's iron and steel mills were important, the city's farm implement manufacturers as well as its railroads being significant consumers of

FIGURE 4. Chicago's Elevated Railroad, Wabash Avenue north from Van Buren Street, ca. 1910.

alleled the two branches of the Chicago River, distributed food and household wares throughout the core Middle West, but also far to the west. Chicago was in competition with other so-called "gateway" cities, including Minneapolis, St. Paul, Omaha, and Kansas City, that funneled agricultural products into and finished goods out of the industrial Northeast. By 1900, American industry was located mainly in a zone extending from Minneapolis–St. Paul and Kansas City on the west to Baltimore, Philadelphia, New York City, and Boston on the east, the so-called "Manufacturing Belt." It was there that the vast majority of Americans resided.

Retailing in Chicago thrived downtown in the area known as the "Loop," so named for the circuit of the elevated railroad built in the 1890s above Wabash, Lake, Wells, and Van Buren Streets (**FIGURE 4**). State Street, however, evolved as the city's main retail thoroughfare. The city's principal retailers were clustered there, including its giant department stores, a retailing venue that was substantially pioneered by Chicagoans. Two blocks to the east on Michigan Avenue, where both wealthy Chicagoans and visitors to the city shopped for high-style fashions, retailing emulated New York City's Fifth Avenue, and even London's Regent Street. Mail-order retailing thrived in Chicago as well, thanks to the city's central location in the nation's evolving railroad network; Sears, Roebuck and Company and Montgomery Ward and Company were local businesses that became national household names.

But what truly set Chicago apart from the other large midwestern cities was its strength as a financial center. In 1900, nearly half of the nation's small-city and small-town banks were networked as "correspondents" through Chicago banking houses, two of which, First National and Union National, together held the deposits of some eighty national banks across fifteen states. The majority of the city's financial institutions clustered along

their products. Like grain handling, meat packing, lumber milling, and implement manufacturing, iron and steel production evolved in Chicago as a highly mechanized industrial process. A huge demand for labor was created in the city, especially for unskilled workers who were willing to accept low pay primarily as machine tenders. Chicago and the other industrial cities in the state attracted immigrant workers, especially from northern, central, eastern, and southern Europe.

Chicago became an important wholesaling and retailing center. Warehouses located along the city's railroad lines, especially those that par-

LaSalle Street, Chicago's equivalent to New York City's Wall Street. The Chicago Board of Trade, established in 1848, was especially important. It oversaw and strengthened the city's business life, promoting harbor improvement, the building of a city-wide sewage and drainage system, the establishment of telegraph service, and the charging of canal tolls in order to maintain and improve the Illinois and Michigan Canal. Importantly, it helped lobby for the federal land grant conferred on the Illinois Central Railroad. Its regulatory work was especially beneficial: the board was empowered to create and enforce regulations for grain handling and to arbitrate disputes between grain dealers. But it was the creation of the "futures market" that had the greatest impact. Through the instrument of the "grain future," a negotiable monetary instrument, grain and other commodities could be placed in speculation.

Chicago excelled in a host of activities, in some of which it was either the second- or the third-most important city nationally. In publishing, Chicago ranked second in value produced, but in actual volume of printed material it was first. Books, magazines, and catalogs might be edited in New York City, but they tended to be printed in and distributed from Chicago. Given the city's central location, printed materials could be rapidly delivered by mail nationwide.

Chicago was not the only city at midcontinent that seemed to be destined for greatness. Indeed, preeminence could easily have fallen to St. Louis instead. St. Louis had controlled the fur trade, the most important economic activity in the region from the French period through the 1820s. It was the older city, having been founded some two decades before Chicago's first settler (fur trader Jean Baptiste Point du Sable) located along the Chicago River. St. Louis remained the larger place through the 1870s. In retrospect, St. Louis became overly dependent on steamboat technology, serving as a point of exchange between two steamboat fleets (shallow-draft boats on the rivers upstream from the city and deep-draft boats downstream). The city's trade was accordingly oriented largely north and south. Chicago's advantage lay primarily in trade east and west. Once eastern trunk-line railroads reached Chicago in the 1850s, the economy of the Midwest became fully integrated with that of the Northeast. East St. Louis, opposite St. Louis on the Illinois side of the Mississippi River, evolved as an industrial satellite of St. Louis (FIGURE 5). Trunk railroads extended branch lines to East St. Louis, offering a belated connection eastward. Massive rail yards and freight houses came to dominate the city's waterfront.

The German economist Johann Heinrich von Thünen's central place theory helps to explain both the commercial reach of large cities such as Chicago and St. Louis and the spacing and somewhat hierarchical sizing of lesser urban places within large-city trade hinterlands. By 1910, Chicago was more than twice as large as St. Louis, and several times larger than Milwaukee, Minneapolis, Kansas City, or any of the other metropolitan areas nested within its sphere of influence. Smaller than Chicago by at least half (Peoria and Rockford), and then smaller by at least another half still (Springfield, Bloomington-Normal, Rock Island), were Illinois cities distanced from one another at intervals varying from 50 to 100 miles. Within their hinterlands clustered even smaller cities, and within their spheres of influence, in turn, were small towns down to the smallest villages and hamlets. Larger urban centers contained most, if not all, of the economic and cultural functions found in the smaller places subsidiary to them: what the smaller centers did, the larger centers above them did as well. But as one went higher up the urban hierarchy, specialization was increasingly encountered, not only in retailing but also in industrial employment.

High Water, East St. Louis, Ill.

FIGURE 5. The Mississippi River in flood, East St. Louis, ca. 1910.

Among the more prominent downstate cities was Springfield, which was chosen as the state capital in 1837, being located only twenty miles from the state's geographic center. But it was Peoria and Rockford that subsequently competed to be the state's second-largest urban place. Both cities evolved as important industrial centers: distilling and implement manufacture at Peoria and machine-tool and hardware manufacture at Rockford. No single city came to fully dominate central Illinois; rather, many separate cities emerged: Springfield and Peoria, as well as Bloomington-Normal, Champaign-Urbana, and Decatur. Rock Island in far west-central Illinois grew as part of a large conurbation with neighboring Moline and East Moline in Illinois and Davenport across the Mississippi River in Iowa. FIGURE 6 shows Rock Island's principal retail street on the morning of a circus parade, such events being ideal settings for illustrating a city's vitality in postcard art.

Well down the urban hierarchy were the courthouse towns, the numerous farm towns (as well as smaller farm villages and hamlets), and the mining towns, such as Christopher, Du Quoin, West Frankfort, and Benton in the southern Illinois coal field. Most of the state's small towns were in fact farm towns, located along one of the many railroad lines. As the railroads covered the state in a dense but somewhat orderly network, and since the topography throughout much of the state was relatively flat and thus not a hindrance to railroad construction, the spacing between towns of varying sizes was quite regular. It might be said that von Thünen's idealized ordering of urban places substantially applied. It was to a railroad siding that farm families went to market their produce,

FIGURE 6. Circus parade, Rock Island, ca. 1910.

and it was with nearby main street merchants that they did their shopping.

Chicago, too, was spatially structured with some regularity, especially in regard to retailing. Like all cities, it was anchored by a large central business district, with lesser business areas spaced at regular intervals outward across its grid of streets, particularly where key streetcar or mass transit lines intersected. Commercial strips evolved along streetcar routes, later reinforced by auto use. Additionally, the city was partitioned into neighborhoods: residential districts separated not only by railroad rights-of-way and their adjacent industrial land areas, but also by major thoroughfares. Various sections of the city took on very different personalities as city residents sorted themselves out by social class and status, as well as by ethnicity and race.

The "Great Chicago Fire" of 1871 attracted national attention for its devastation of the central city, including the entire downtown business district. The rebuilding of the central district wrought important architectural innovation. Balloon framing (the use of light lumber instead of heavy timbers for framing houses and other buildings) had become synonymous with Chicago ingenuity when it was introduced in the city in the 1830s. After the fire, the city council banned wood construction of all kinds downtown, an action that increased the use of masonry, and then invited the use of iron and steel, especially in the erection of tall buildings. Giant metal frames made it possible for buildings to achieve great heights at relatively low cost, an important development given Chicago's escalating land values inside the Loop (**FIGURE 7**). Skeletal framing replaced

FIGURE 7. A view over Chicago's central business district, 1900.

heavy masonry for load-bearing walls and could be more easily sheathed in glass, thus opening up building interiors to exterior light. With the addition of innovations such as elevators, electric lighting, and modern plumbing, the modern skyscraper was born.

A city's functionality reflected ease and speed of movement. What elevators did for Chicago's tall buildings, mass transit accomplished for the city as a whole. Eighteen horse-drawn omnibus lines served the city in 1865, making it possible to commute to work over relatively long distances. They were followed by cable cars, elevated steam-powered trains, elevated electric trains (some of which served the Loop by subway tunnel), electric streetcars, and finally buses. The city's boundaries were increasingly pushed outward as new transit lines developed and as the railroads began to offer commuter service. The extension of city water and sewer services was equally important for urban growth, as was the extension of electri-

cal service. But mainly it was transportation that counted: a "star-shaped" metropolis emerged by 1910, reflecting the major lines of transportation that radiated outward from the city's center before the auto age.

The World's Columbian Exposition of 1893 enabled Chicago boosters to promote their city on a world stage: to foster a positive image very much of their own making. While they could mask many of the social problems that festered in the city, especially in the badly blighted older neighborhoods into which increasing numbers of in-migrants crowded, they could not solve them. Critics noted the sharp contrast between the exposition grounds and older, poorer sections of the city. But they also decried the apparent sameness of the city's newer areas, with mile after mile of seemingly look-alike tenements and workers' cottages. They deplored the impersonality of the large factory floors. The exposition offered visitors a kind of fairyland. It was quintessentially a visual event,

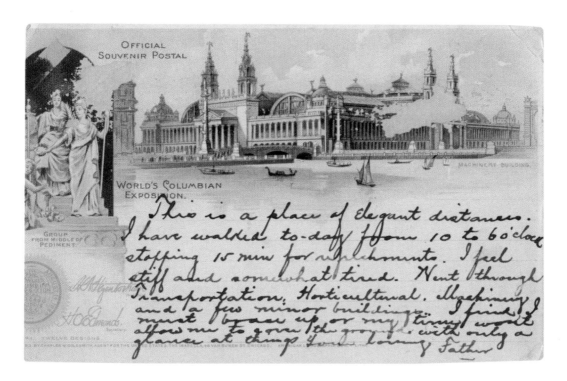

FIGURE 8. Official Souvenir Postal Card, World's Columbian Exposition, 1893.

fully suggestive of Chicago's, and the nation's, potential for perfection. "Make no little plans; they have no magic to stir men's blood," said Daniel Burnham, who was the director of works for the exposition. Burnham assembled a notable group of architects and artists to create the "White City," in which exhibition buildings, covered largely in white plaster of Paris and constructed mostly in the Beaux Arts style of European classicism, were arranged formally around ceremonial plazas with reflecting pools. As a gigantic set piece, the fair dazzled. It stood dramatically as a kind of theater, especially when electrically illuminated at night.

Depicted in FIGURE 8 is a forerunner of the picture postcard: a "postal card" that was sold at the 1893 World's Columbian Exposition. Before commercially published postcards were legalized, only official postal cards, issued in bulk by the United States Postal Service itself, could be sent through the U.S. mail. This card, therefore, was one of the very first with a scenic view available for individuals to purchase. It features the fair's Government Building, located on the formal Court of Honor. The Exposition Board, headed by architect Burnham, mandated a white "Greco-Roman" complex of monumental, temple-like buildings, its open spaces formally outlined in arrays of columns, pilasters, and arches. More than 27 million people visited the fair.

Initially, at least, most visitors to the exposition were impressed by its size and its classical formality. Displays in the giant exhibition halls highlighted the nation's technical, commercial, and even artistic triumphs. At first glance, the fairgrounds seemed to offer a welcomed lesson in city planning. But after a while, many fairgoers came to feel otherwise. Like the person who wrote the message across the front of the card in FIGURE 8, they found the White City overly large and a challenge to get around on foot. They found it visually tiring as well, because of the sameness and strict orderliness of its highly predicable landscape. The entertainment zone, the so-called "Midway Plaisance," quickly captured visitors' attention with its thrill rides and its carnival attractions. Most visitors, it seemed, preferred a good time to an education.

One of the exposition's lasting legacies came fifteen years later, when Burnham and his assistant, Edward H. Bennett, prepared the *Plan of Chicago* for a group of elite city boosters. Although it was never fully implemented, it remained a celebrated city-planning document, energizing a nationwide "City Beautiful" movement that resulted in new civic centers and boulevarded streets in cities across the United States. Upon the heels of this belated Beaux Arts vision came the work of Frank Lloyd Wright, promoter of the so-called "Prairie School" of architecture, an embrace of design ideas incubated by Louis H. Sullivan, with whom Wright had initially worked. A distinctly Middle Western look was sought: buildings of low silhouette with strongly emphasized horizontal lines, buildings where indoors and outdoors seemed to flow together, and buildings where the use of natural materials predominated in symbolizing a closeness with nature. It was a look that rejected traditional design antecedents, and thereby anticipated modernism. While it was never popularly embraced, Wrightian experimentation was at least something that Chicagoans and Illinoisans could later take pride in as being regionally based.

Parks also set Chicago apart from most other American cities. A ring of large parks (including Jackson Park, where the World's Columbian Exposition had been located) were connected by well-landscaped parkways, along many of which the more affluent families built large houses. The city's entire Lake Michigan shoreline was ultimately landscaped as park space, although after World War II, Lake Shore (or Outer) Drive was converted into a high-speed freeway. Park and garden designs were allied with the "prairie" theme in architecture, especially those by landscape gardener Jens Jensen. Oriented to Lincoln Park along the lakefront north of the Loop were the city's finest townhouses, and later its finest apartment towers, in an area called the "Gold Coast." As mass transit and railroad commuting opened up the Lake Michigan shore farther and farther to the north, upscale suburbs evolved, including Evanston, Kenilworth, Winnetka, Wilmette, and Lake Forest.

Demographically, Chicago bore a distinctly Yankee imprint, especially among the upper classes. Many of the city's well-to-do families originated in New England and Upstate New York. Southern Illinois, in contrast, was settled mainly by people from the Upper South: from Kentucky or Tennessee, with roots in Virginia or North Carolina. Central Illinois was more mixed, with migrants from the Upper South and some from New England, but also from Indiana and Ohio, people who were part of a multigenerational migration stream rooted originally in Pennsylvania and New Jersey. Scattered throughout the state, both in rural areas and in the towns and cities, were the foreign-born, most numerous those of German, Irish, and Scandinavian origins.

German-speaking immigrants and their children, including those born in the United States, made up one-sixth of Chicago's population in 1850. The German American population, as well as the large Czech American population in the city, included not only the working poor, but an affluent merchant class as well. The Irish, however, tended more to the laboring classes, as did the Poles and Russian Jews. The Irish were initially attracted to work on the Illinois and Michigan Canal, and accordingly came to cluster residentially near the canal in the Bridgeport neighborhood. Poles supplied much of the labor for the city's stockyards, giving Chicago the second-largest Polish population behind Warsaw. It also had the second-largest Swedish population behind Stockholm. At first the Jewish community in Chicago consisted largely of affluent merchant families. In the 1880s, however, an influx of largely impoverished and Yiddish-speaking Jews from central and eastern Europe began to cluster on the city's near west side, especially around Maxwell Street, with Italians and Greeks locating there as well.

Both native-born and immigrant families tended to move out from the center of the city as they grew more affluent, settling in newer, and invariably better, neighborhoods. The city grew incrementally, with concentric rings of growth expanding outward decade by decade. Close to the Loop, older residential neighborhoods gave way to warehousing and small factories as commerce had a blighting effect on housing stock, most of it rental property. The landlord class, in speculating on increased real estate values, tended to disinvest old houses, while at the same time dividing them up into multiple units in order to extract maximum rent. The city's older neighborhoods thus became rundown and overcrowded, especially where tenants, such as the city's African Americans, were concentrated. Blacks were severely restricted as to where they could reside, racism being flagrant. After the Civil War, the city's black population concentrated mainly on the city's near south side, the so-called "Black Metropolis," rapidly increasing in size during and after World War I as migrants from both the Upper and the Lower South came seeking factory work.

Located on the near south side was the Levee, the city's principal "illicit" zone, known for gambling, prostitution, and drug-dealing. It was here,

during Prohibition, that organized crime brought Al Capone and his cronies to world attention. Capone remains Chicago's most famous (or infamous) native son. Civic strife, like crime, always lay just below the seemingly placid surface of everyday life in Chicago, and beyond the metropolis as well, especially in the coal towns. Malady was predicated not just on recognized social inequality but on the inability of many working people, especially during hard economic times, to obtain decent wages, and thus to provide for even basic family needs. Labor-management disputes escalated to widely publicized violence during the Railroad Strike of 1877, and again during the Haymarket Affair of 1886. Corruption marred municipal governance in Chicago as it did in most cities where political "machines" operated unfettered.

Despite the city's social problems and frequent political malaise, life in Chicago nonetheless symbolized a kind of progress to most Americans. But so did life as it was lived beyond the metropolis. By 1910, farmers in east-central Illinois, for example, were turning from general farming, with an emphasis on both livestock and grain, to grain farming exclusively. The region's flat terrain, not to mention its rich soils, invited mechanization, first with giant steam tractors that specialized crews used in planting and harvesting crops, and then with gasoline-powered tractors that farmers could afford on their own and operate by themselves. The motor truck was an important new means for farmers to get crops to market, thus ending the near-monopoly that the railroads had held on long-distance shipping. Mechanization reduced labor costs, making crops cheaper to produce. Thus farmers, at least those who were able to afford the new machines as well as the additional land to make their use fully profitable, were able to survive the declining crop prices that caused problems for farmers nationwide, especially after World War I.

As part of the Old Northwest, Illinois was a "free soil" state, slavery being prohibited. When public lands were surveyed, they were divided off by range and township lines, and then by section lines, into mile-square tracts. As the nineteenth century progressed, public land was sold in smaller and smaller parcels to individuals, and on increasingly liberal terms. What Thomas Jefferson had envisioned as a kind of political ideal was largely realized: an American population, made up substantially of landowners, that would firmly support an active and effective democracy.

By 1910, however, most Illinois farm families were tenants rather than landowners. And by 1960, farm consolidation had left relatively few farm families on the land as either owners or tenants; like nearly every other commercial enterprise, farming had become big business. Cash grain farms, for example, needed to be large (upwards of 300 acres) in order to remain profitable. Increasingly larger and thus more expensive tractors, planters, and harvesters had to be bought. Only the most entrepreneurial farmers survived. A new petroleum-based agriculture evolved, one that relied not just on giant machines and the fuel that made them run, but on new plant seeds genetically engineered to be used with the new petroleum-derived fertilizers and herbicides. Rural populations declined.

The automobile altered small towns. If small-towners and farm families could get to town easily and quickly, they could also get easily and quickly to the cities, where stores were both more numerous and bigger, thus carrying a wider range of merchandise at lower prices. After World War I, the smallest hamlets and villages across Illinois began to lose their retailing; thereafter, town functions were steadily transferred up the urban hierarchy to larger and larger places. In 1950, Chicago had a population of 3,620,926, a decline of 9 percent over the previous decade. Nonetheless, it was still the nation's second-largest city. In 1950, approximately 81 percent of Illinoisans lived in urban centers, and only 19 percent in rural areas; 51 of the state's 102 counties had lost population during the decade.

POSTCARD PUBLISHERS

Postal cards, which were sold exclusively by the U.S. Postal Service, were popularized beginning in the 1860s. Sent mainly by businesses as advertising, they could be bought and mailed only in bulk. Postcards, so called to distinguish them from postal cards, were legalized only in 1893. They could be bought and mailed individually by individuals. European nations were faster off the mark, giving postcard publishers, especially in Germany, Austria, and Switzerland, an important head start. Through the 1930s, the highest-quality view cards available in the United States were invariably printed in Europe. Chicago helped pioneer the picture postcard in the United States when in 1893 the European practice of issuing postcard views of official trade exhibitions was adopted for the World's Columbian Exposition. Indeed, it was Charles W. Goldsmith, a Chicagoan, who put on sale a set of ten postcards illustrating various buildings at the fair, printed by the American Lithograph Company of New York City.

While Chicago did not dominate the picture postcard trade nationally, the city's postcard publishers exerted substantial influence nationwide. At first, the postcard business in Chicago involved mainly distribution. With the cards being printed overseas, postcard publishers functioned as wholesalers, distributing cards across sales territories of varying extent. However, Chicago firms did supply the illustrative material to be printed, gearing it to local market tastes. Early in the twentieth century, Chicago publishers such as Alfred Holzmann dominated postcard sales both in the city and beyond the metropolis.

FACTORY OF ALFRED HOLZMAN COMPANY, CHICAGO
The largest building in America devoted exclusively to the manufacture of Post Cards

FIGURE 9. Advertising postcard for the Alfred Holzmann Company, Chicago, ca. 1915.

FIGURE 9 shows an advertising postcard issued by the Holzmann firm featuring a view of its own printing plant (identified as "The largest building in America devoted exclusively to the manufacture of Post Cards"). On the back, partially preprinted and partially handwritten, is the message: "We are in receipt of your valued order of 12-2-00. Why not get out post cards of this kind with your factory on?" The card was addressed to the Imperial Glass Company, Charleroi, Pennsylvania. From the 1930s through the 1950s, Chicago's Curt Teich and Company was the nation's largest postcard publisher. But publishers in other cities were also important over the decades in picturing Chicago and Illinois beyond the metropolis, among them Hugh C. Leighton of Portland, Maine, the Detroit Publishing Company of Detroit, L. L. Cook of Milwaukee, and even the Raphael Tuck Company of London.

The Detroit Publishing Company cards were perhaps the finest ever made (see figure 7). They were printed through a patented "photochrome" process that had been developed in Switzerland. They were not color photographs, although their image quality anticipated color photography. Nor were they the usual halftone prints that enabled black-and-white photo images to be color-printed through multiple press runs, usually in four hues. They were continuous-tone color renditions of single black-and-white photos, but produced through the multiple impressions of photolithographic plates, upwards of a dozen in number. The Raphael Tuck Company, for its part, began to produce greeting cards in the 1870s, and later, as a logical outgrowth of that business, built a notable line of high-quality postcards. Next to view cards, postcards featuring holiday greetings were the most numerous in the United States.

The Payne-Aldrich Tariff Act of 1909 set high tax rates on printed materials imported from abroad, eventually leading America's postcard publishers to either manufacture their own cards, handle cards manufactured domestically by others, or drop out of the business. Many became retailers. In Chicago, several bookstores were converted exclusively to postcard sales. But most early picture postcards were sold at drugstores, railroad stations, hotels, and tourist attractions. By 1920, postcard racks could be found in a wide variety of retail establishments, from dime stores to department stores. At the wholesale level, 119 Chicago postcard distributers (including manufacturers) appear in the business directories and telephone books of the city between 1900 and 1930. The products of twenty-seven of them are displayed in this book (see the list of credits).

Among the first Chicago postcard suppliers was Victor O. Hammon, who started business in Minneapolis in 1904, expanding to Chicago the following year (see figure 4). In 1906 he moved his personal residence to the city. Superlatively printed and colored view cards made up most of the V. O. Hammon Company's inventory, although cheap gimmickry entered on occasion. In 1909, the firm printed a series of "jigsaw cards" whose precut pieces could be sent in an envelope for the recipient to piece back together.

Most of the city's postcard publishers, including the Gerson Brothers, C. R. Childs, and S. H. Knox, were originally located in or at the edge of Chicago's downtown. But by 1920, especially those firms engaged in the actual printing of cards had shifted their facilities well beyond the Loop, most to one or another of the city's industrial zones. The largest postcard printing plant ever built in the city was opened well north of downtown by Curt Teich in the 1920s. Teich was a German immigrant who had entered the printing business with rail-road-oriented products similar to those produced by Rand McNally. While the latter firm turned to publishing road maps, Curt Teich turned to publishing postcards. In 1904, following a sojourn in Germany, where he improved his printing skills, Teich returned to the United States, traveling for several months to photograph views and line up local retailers for his postcard line. He was among the first in the United States, and was the very first in Chicago, to produce colored postcards on an offset press, which, by substantially reducing his costs, gave him a clear market advantage. His process was eventually adopted nationwide.

In the 1930s, Curt Teich and Company also pioneered cards with a "linen" finish, so named because the texture and pattern of the paper used to make them resembled linen fabric. Such is the advertising card in FIGURE 10, printed by Teich for Chicago's Hotel Continental. The view here is south over the city's downtown, with Grant Park in the distance depicted in a soft pastoral green. Such cards were very colorful, but also quite visibly retouched, with unnecessary detail removed to "clean" or simplify an image. Through World War II, Curt Teich employed some 1,000 workers, including 100 artists.

National postcard companies, including those located in Chicago, entered mainly big-city markets to sell mainly big-city views. One exception was Curt Teich, which produced postcards picturing all of Illinois's downstate tourist attractions, all of its small-city downtowns, and many of its small-town main streets as well. Another company, L. L. Cook of Milwaukee, specialized in black-and-white "real photo" views of small towns. Also numerous, at least on postcard racks beyond the metropolis, were black-and-white photo postcards produced by local commercial portrait photographers who were interested in broadening their customer base.

FIGURE 10. Advertising postcard for the Hotel Continental, Chicago, ca. 1940.

Also included in this book are selected snapshot views taken by, and mainly printed by, amateur photographers. In 1902, the Eastman Kodak Company introduced postcard-sized silver chloride photo papers on which amateurs, as well as professionals, could print images from negatives under ordinary light. Photo chemistry was simple enough that negatives and prints could easily be developed in a darkened hotel restroom, thus providing "instant" souvenirs. Photo paper did not even require chemical fixing. These views were highly personalized, to say the least—views to be mailed to friends and relatives to update them on one's travels, for example. The area on the back of each card was divided, with equal space for an address and for a message. The requisite "postcard" designation required by the postal service was printed along the top.

In **FIGURE 11**, a family in their new Ford Model T is heading out to watch the University of Chicago's football team play on a sunny Saturday afternoon in the fall of 1915. The husband and wife, Grant and Emily Thornton, were both teachers at the Chicago Parental School, a city-run school for delinquent boys. The Thorntons were from the small town of Homer in Champaign County, located not far from Champaign-Urbana. Both were avid amateur photographers. Pictures of people dominated amateur snapshot photography, especially pictures taken during important family events or during times of leisure such as Labor Day or Fourth of July celebrations. Frequently photographed also were houses, their front porches, their yards, and the residential streets along which they were located, both in towns and in cities. There were numerous snapshots of farm

FIGURE 11. A football weekend at the University of Chicago, ca. 1915.

life made by farm people. Amateur cards added to the flood of commercial postcard art entering the mails. They contributed substantially to the postcard iconography by which Chicago and Illinois beyond the metropolis came to be visualized.

Amateur photography fully dominated in one important place: the snapshot albums that most American families kept on their parlor tables. Many people regularly exchanged postcards through the mail, storing their trophies in albums or boxing them up when their albums overflowed. Collections that were stored away in attic trunks and other safe locations more than a hundred years ago continue to resurface today, in the same condition and in the same order of presentation as when their original owners put them away for the last time. Collectors also formed postcard clubs, which hosted monthly meetings, and the largest of which sponsored postcard shows and held conventions.

Postcard collecting is still popular, although on a much smaller scale in comparison to early last century. Today vintage postcard art tends to be valued as a historical form of visual culture, with rare cards commanding high prices. Of importance to aficionados of Chicago and Illinois history beyond the metropolis, however, is what postcards tell us about the past—both the past as it actually was and the past as it was once imagined to be. A vintage view provides a window back in time, in a sense a portal through which today's views might step to survey and assess. Of course, not everything of importance in the past lent itself to postcard imagery. The view backward through any medium is always skewed.

What was emphasized in postcard views was history translated into material culture—especially history as implicated in things architectural or, perhaps better said, at the scale of landscape. Emphasized were what might be termed "icons" of place that translated history into geography. Each postcard publisher's array of images created an iconography in which depictions of the built environment (and sometimes the natural environment as well) combined to visually represent localities. Publishers also sought to picture important events or ongoing activities—history in the making, so to speak. But mainly it was history hardened into geography—places viewed as deriving over time through one or another process of change.

Picture postcards have too often been dismissed as objects of fleeting value lacking serious intent beyond a personal message between friends. "Hello! Wish you were here"—the picture of the postcard showing a scene beautified for consumption without question. In fact, picture postcards structured how and what views were to be taken from a rapidly changing world. They were an effective means to these ends because they were themselves novel and impacted viewers widely through visual and popular culture. Illinois's history, its sense of an evolving landscape and place, were given to be understood through postcard art; this was no small undertaking. Chicago, a publishing and printing center, not only produced many postcards but was itself their subject—an international "boom town." Illinois beyond the metropolis was to be taken for a national heartland and the cradle of Lincoln's greatness, the "Land of Lincoln." People viewing postcards of these subjects literally envisioned and thereby reflexively adapted their geography of Illinois.

PART ONE

Chicago and Its Suburbs: The Metropolis

FIGURE 12. Novelty postcard, ca. 1946.

As the nation's boom metropolis, Chicago was a major tourist attraction, and a major source of pride to its residents. "Greetings from Chicago" was a thought, if not an actual phrase used, resonating with all the many postcards sent and received from the city early in the twentieth century. The caption on the novelty card in **FIGURE 12** reads in part: "Chicago, Miracle City of the Age in little

FIGURE 13. A view over Chicago's central business district, ca. 1935.

more than 100 years, grew from a village of a few log cabins to the fourth largest city on the globe." The French had borrowed the word "Che-cau-gou" from native parlance, applying it to the river that, by short portage, strategically connected Lake Michigan with the Des Plaines, Illinois, and Mississippi Rivers. It was a foul-smelling, marshy world of wild leek and skunk cabbage. Chicago's population exploded from some 4,500 people in 1840 to more than 1.7 million in 1900 (with another 400,000 in its suburbs), growing at a rate of some 75,000 each year. The metropolis stretched for more than twenty-five miles along Lake Michigan, and inland away from the lake upwards of twelve miles. "Here, midmost in the land," penned the novelist Frank Norris, "beat the Heart of the Nation, whence inevitably must come its immeasurable power, its infinite, infinite, inexhaustible vitality. Here, of all her cities, throbbed the true life—the true power and spirit of America." Chi-

cago was spoken of in superlatives: "Call Chicago mighty, monstrous, multifarious, vital, lusty, stupendous, indomitable, intense, unnatural, aspiring, puissant, preposterous, transcendent—call it what you like—throw the dictionary at it!" exclaimed the travel writer Julian Street.

Chicago's official motto became "I will," although the city founders had originally adopted *Urbs in horto* (city in a garden) in acknowledgment of the fecundity of the surrounding prairie hinterland. The descriptor "Windy City" became popular in the twentieth century, referencing not only the gales that sometimes raged off of Lake Michigan, but also the ballyhoo with which Chicagoans tended to boast of their city. Postcard publishers played to boosterism, relying on an array of pictorial conventions in doing so. Preferred viewpoints and compositional conventions repeated over and over again in the city's postcard art. For example, distanced views that emphasized the grand while obscuring the menial, especially the untoward, were favored, presenting visual "tableaus" by which the city might be understood and remembered.

Nothing distanced the city better than a "bird's-eye view." "If you look at Chicago from the air," wrote journalists John and Ruth Ashenhurst, "you will see how it is divided into segments by the railroad lines which converge upon its central district, cutting great gashes through the city's roofs like the fingers of a hand or the ribs of a fan. Contrasting with these are the twin ribbons of the Chicago River diverging outward to the northwest and southwest from the fork, half a mile west of the lake front." The view in FIGURE 13 is out over the Chicago River just west of the lakefront, the array of skyscrapers along North Michigan Avenue disrupted by the river, with the avenue's bridge as a focal point. It was there—the site of Fort Dearborn—that, a century earlier, Chicago had its start as a city. "The city has a surprising beauty," journalist Graham Hutton observed. "The beauty shines through all of its grime, the dirt of hard work. I have stood many a time, of a fall evening or in the depth of terrible winters, on the Michigan Avenue Bridge and looked west to see the girders of the many bridges over the Chicago River and the skyscrapers and the sunset beyond; and I have wondered why a Midwest school of painting did not spring up here."

FIGURE 14A. State Street, ca. 1925.

STATE STREET AND THE LOOP

Following the fire of 1871, State Street became the city's principal retail street, and thus the symbolic center of downtown. FIGURE 14A shows a view taken about 1925 south along State Street, with the eye directed to architect Louis H. Sullivan's celebrated Schlesinger and Mayer Department Store (later Carson, Pirie, Scott and Company), located at what was claimed to be "The Busiest Corner in the World." The caption reads: "It is said that more people pass this corner in 24 hours than any other spot in the world." A sense of linear perspective, exaggerated through the visual compression of a telephoto lens, is enhanced by the photographer's attention to composition. Carefully integrated are the streetcar tracks, the streetlights, and the building facades, which, in elbowing one another, appear to recede in the distance. Although the camera was slightly elevated, the view that is communicated here is essentially what a pedestrian

359. STATE STREET, LOOKING NORTH FROM VAN BUREN STREET, CHICAGO.

50359

FIGURE 14B. State Street north from Van Buren Street, ca. 1915.

would have seen from the sidewalk. It was the kind of view by which people early in the twentieth century tended to know cities: the open vista of a street with building facades obliquely viewed in passing. A sense of movement is implied, with the viewer pulled into the scene as an active onlooker.

The view in FIGURE 14B, taken a decade earlier, is looking in the opposite direction, showing the street less congested but the sidewalks equally packed. State Street was the shopping artery that Chicagoans knew best, and the one that visitors invariably sought out. Its imagery was iconographic, standing not just for the thoroughfare itself, but for the city as a whole. Pictures such as this taught not only what Chicago looked like but how it ought to be looked at and remembered. They helped set the city apart as a distinctive place.

People moved on the public way. Sidewalks also had to provide space for those who stopped

to linger, if only to browse a store's display windows (FIGURE 15). The prospect of the open vista in movement was important, but so was the sense of refuge that being at rest implied. By stepping through a doorway into a store, a pedestrian could escape from the "madding crowd." Building fronts were designed to attract attention and thus invite people inside, marking them as desirable destinations. At S. H. Knox's Five and Ten Cent Store, a large sign, easily readable even from across the street, stretched the length of the building's facade. Merchandise displayed in the large windows was suggestive of what was offered inside. Entry was made by two large doors, both reinforced by secondary signs. Such places, defined at the scale of the store, could be found all along State Street. They were what the street was all about. Places might be thought of as behavior settings that nest in landscape. They are variously centers of inter-

26] Part One

FIGURE 15. State Street, ca. 1905.

est toward which people are potentially attracted, or indeed from which they are repelled, according to their needs and intentions of the moment. Of course, the street itself was also a kind of place, but one that postcard photographers pictured and interpreted more at the scale of landscape.

Department stores were especially important for women, particularly the wives and daughters of upper-middle- and upper-class families who could afford the time and the money to shop in these places of enhanced aesthetic appeal and heightened safety. But they were also important to the working-class women who hired on as sales clerks. Despite long hours and often difficult working conditions, young women of the lower classes flocked to clerking and clerical work that offered a kind of "white-collar" or middle-class respectability. Marshall Field's (**FIGURE 16**) treated its customers grandly: "Give the Lady What She Wants" was

the store motto, and that included not just linen handkerchiefs, kid gloves, boxes of chocolates, and bottles of perfume, but everything imaginable in the way of millinery, clothing, home furnishings, appliances, and even groceries. Marion Louise Wineman described Chicago's "Ladies' Mile" at the close of day:

> The Bell in the clock of the Boston Store
> Tolls sweet on the evening air,
> For homewending stenos and clerks galore,
> And a few hundred thousand or maybe more
> Weary shoppers from Field's and the Fair.

"Of course we visited Marshall Field's," Julian Street emphasized. He was escorted by an assistant manager in and out of "baffling doors and passageways" from the public parts of the store, where goods were sold, to areas very much "behind the scenes." They went "through great rooms

FIGURE 16. Marshall Field's Department Store, ca. 1915.

FIGURE 17. Atrium at Marshall Field's, ca. 1910.

full of trunks, of brass beds, through vast galleries of furniture, through restaurants, grilles, afternoon tea rooms, rooms full of curtain and coverings and cushions and corsets and waists and hats and carpets and rugs and linoleum and lamps and toys and stationery and silver, and Heaven only knows what else," he wrote. Marshall Field's even had its own telegraph office and post office. The store occupied two separate buildings, which were added to incrementally over several decades. Both of the main sections faced State Street, each centered on a large interior atrium. In FIGURE 17, one of those atriums is decorated for the holiday season. It was topped, like its twin, by a Tiffany glass mosaic backlit by a skylight. A dramatic multistory space, it effectively oriented customers as they worked their way up or down, floor by floor, through the store. The building's decor carried classical implications both inside and out: from the huge Ionic porticos at the State Street entrances, through the columned arcades of the atriums, to the columns used as ceiling supports on virtually every sales floor.

Like other department stores along State Street, Marshall Field's had multiple basements (**FIGURE 18**). There was a bargain basement for remaindered goods offered at discounted prices. Lower down was where new merchandise arrived, and where customer purchases were packaged for delivery across the city, or for shipment across the Midwest or even nationwide. Farther down still was much of the equipment used to distribute electrical power, water, and heat throughout the building. Each of the two buildings in which the store was housed had its own heavy metal frame. Weight was carried down through steel columns to caissons driven deep into the ground. Postcards routinely pictured what needed to be seen in a city, but some, such as this card, also depicted what most people would likely never see, but needed, nonetheless, to visualize and thus understand. Such cards played to the American penchant to know how things worked. They were also meant to impress people with the progress and technical sophistication they showed.

A sixty-mile system of freight tunnels beneath the streets of Chicago's downtown was completed in 1909 (**FIGURE 19**). Its narrow-gage electric railway, with some 132 locomotives and some 3,000 cars, connected major downtown buildings, coal being the most important cargo carried in, and ash, from boilers and furnaces, the most important thing carried out. But the package freight was also significant; Marshall Field's sub-sub-basement, for example, was directly connected to a tunnel so that customer purchases could be quickly shipped out. Not only did the tunnels speed delivery, in that freight bypassed the street congestion above, but they also substantially reduced that congestion. An estimated 5,000 truck trips were thereby eliminated daily. With the trains operating ten hours a day, there was, on average, one train moving every minute. The tunnels were six feet wide and seven and a

FIGURE 18. Diagram of Marshall Field's below ground, ca. 1910.

half feet high, and made of steel-reinforced concrete "12 inches thick all around." No other city had such a system.

"With your eyes peppered with dust, with your ears full of the clatter of the Elevated Road, and with the prairie breezes playfully buffeting you and waltzing with you by turns, as they eddy through the ravines of Madison Avenue, or Adams-street, you take your life in your hand when you attempt the crossing of State-street,

FIGURE 19. Underground freight tunnel, Chicago, ca. 1915.

with its endless stream of rattling waggons and clanging trolley-cars." So wrote the English visitor William Archer. And so it was, he thought, with virtually every street in the Chicago Loop. "New York does not for a moment compare with Chicago in the roar and bustle and bewilderment of its street life," he claimed. The need for underground freight haulage was readily apparent in postcard views such as **FIGURES 20A AND 20B**. On downtown streets, the clatter of horses' hooves, the grind of metal wheels on the pavement, the ring of cable car and streetcar bells, the blare of auto horns, and the shouts of teamsters, peddlers, and newspaper hawkers combined to create an almost unbelievable din. Additionally, there were the odors of horse manure and auto exhaust. In the winter, especially, there was coal smoke. Of course, those were things that, although not seen,

were sensed, aspects of place that could only be implied from pictures.

Chicago had been very much a "walking city" through the 1860s, with most people conditioned to getting places on foot. Mass transit made it even more so, except that some commuters and shoppers rode into the city to walk. Poor drainage prompted the raising of street levels and, of course, the paving of both streets and sidewalks. Tracks were laid out midstreet along which horse-drawn omnibuses could run. The granting of transit franchises was integrally linked with city politics, especially with the coming of cable cars in the 1860s and then electric trolleys in the 1890s. Much corruption in city government hinged on payoffs received from private transit interests. Chicago's first elevated transit lines, placed in operation in 1892 with steam engines, were joined in a loop

FIGURE 20A. Dearborn Street at Randolph Street, ca. 1905.

FIGURE 20B. Adams Street east from State Street, ca. 1900.

FIGURE 21. Elevated Railroad above Wabash Avenue, ca. 1910.

around downtown in 1897, which led Chicagoans to refer to the downtown area as "the Loop" (**FIGURE 21**; see also figure 4). The system was electrified a year later under the direction of transit mogul Charles T. Yerkes. The "el" was an important part of the downtown spectacle; trains passed overhead every two minutes on average during rush hours. In addition, twenty of the city's steam railroads provided passenger service to outlying suburbs. For habitual riders, the railroads discounted or "commuted" ticket prices, thus giving rise to the term "commuter."

During the el's construction, prefabricated pieces of the massive superstructure were hauled to the city center, stacked along the intended rights-of-way, and then raised and bolted together, not unlike a gigantic erector set. Because of the shadows it cast on the streets below, as well as the dust and dirt constantly dislodged by pass-

ing trains, real estate development along Wabash, Lake, Wells, and Van Buren Streets was modest, with most of the city's tall office buildings built on streets away from the elevated lines. Through the 1920s, Wabash remained a street of older, lowrise buildings that housed furniture and piano stores as well as carriage and bicycle shops. "Only a block behind the bright facade of Michigan Avenue," essayist Christopher Morley observed, "you come to the dense and gloomy regions of the Loop. Sometimes in its darker shadows, under the L trestles and where the trolley tracks are set in slippery pink stone chosen for skidding surface, the word Loop seems hardly constricted enough. It might almost be Noose." There, he added, Chicago seemed older than any part of New York. Indeed, it was more like London.

The first subway opened in 1945 and ran under State Street, the busiest of the city's north-south

FIGURE 22. State Street subway, ca. 1945.

elevated lines being reoriented to it (FIGURE 22). A second subway opened under Dearborn Street in 1951. Postcard views of the new underground transit lines spoke clearly of modernity through technological progress. Things were certainly brighter and cleaner there, although perhaps not as picturesque as street-side. In 1947 there were still some 3,500 streetcars, augmented by more than 1,000 buses. But within a decade, the trolleys were gone; buses were thought to be less disruptive of traffic (they were not, after all, restricted to rails at center street), safer (they could pull to the curb to let passengers on and off), and cheaper to operate (in an era of cheap gasoline). Despite the automobile's popularity, Chicago remained a mass transit city, which helped sustain the Loop's viability as an office district through to the twenty-first century.

THE FINANCIAL DISTRICT

As State Street spoke energetically of retailing, so LaSalle Street spoke forcefully of finance: not only banking, but also insurance, brokerage, and, most importantly, trade in agricultural commodities. Around 1910, as pictured in FIGURE 23, LaSalle Street was a scene of architectural experimentation. Buildings variously embraced or rejected traditional architectural massing and ornamentation as architects strove to sort out just what a large office building ought to look like. Frank Norris, in his muckraking novel *The Pit*, described the street at the start of a typical business day: "La Salle Street swarmed with the multitudinous life that seethed about the doors of the innumerable offices of brokers and commission men of the neighbourhood. To the right, in the peristyle of the Illinois Trust Building, groups of clerks, of messengers, of brokers, of clients, and of depositors formed and broke incessantly. To the left, where the facade of the Board of Trade blocked the street, the activity was astonishing, and in and out of the swing doors of its entrances streamed an incessant tide of coming and going."

LA SALLE STREET
CHICAGO

ILLINOIS TRUST
& SAVINGS
BANK
AT RIGHT

FIGURE 23. LaSalle Street, ca. 1910.

Men, he wrote, "mere flotsam in the flood," were swept along in the gathering tides. "At the Illinois Trust the walk became a stride, at the Rookery the stride was almost a trot. But at the corner of Jackson Street . . . the trot became a run, and young men and boys, under the pretence of escaping the trucks and wagons of the cobbles, dashed across at a veritable gallop, flung themselves panting into the entrance of the Board, were engulfed in the turmoil of the spot, and disappeared with a sudden fillip into the gloom of the interior." This was where Chicago and its hinterland came fully together in an economic sense.

As important as bird's-eye views and street scenes were in depicting cities, postcard publishers also favored the direct, head-on picturing of individual buildings. Nothing symbolized a city's economic power quite like its banking community. And nothing symbolized the banking commu-

nity quite like pretentious architecture, including the Illinois Bank and Trust Company's classically styled building, designed by architect Daniel Burnham (**FIGURE 24**). "Bank buildings of the city run mainly to solidity and costliness, with heavy pillars on their fronts," observed Robert Shackleton, who was visiting from England. "There is the Illinois Trust, in its long low building of gray stone, with its nine mighty Corinthian pilasters in the center and half a dozen Corinthian pilasters at either side. And looking down narrow Quincy Street, beside this building, one sees highset pillars above an open balustrade of stone, and, towering far above and behind them, the great dome of the post-office, making in all an impressive vistaed view." A few years before, there had been a freak accident here. A small blimp flying over the city to advertise an amusement park caught fire, exploded, and fell. "The heavy engines, red-

FIGURE 24. Advertising postcard for the Illinois Trust and Savings Bank, ca. 1925.

hot from the gasoline flames, crashed through the glass skylight." Twelve people were killed, John and Ruth Ashenhurst reported.

The Board of Trade was organized to regularize the grain trade, which was especially important to the city. In encouraging the handling of grain in bulk, the board standardized grading and pricing procedures. By 1900, it was the premier commodity exchange in the nation, having innovated the use of buyer "options" that enabled speculation in "futures." Terminating the view south along LaSalle Street, the Board of Trade Building symbolized the power of the city's financial community (FIGURE 25). Eclectic in its ornamental detail, the building was massive in its overall form, its thick load-bearing walls constructed of huge blocks of Maine granite. At the top of the structure, an outdoor viewing platform offered an exceptional view down and across the city. Visitors entered the main entrance through a portico framed by squared-off columns topped by large lintels crowned with allegorical figures representing agriculture and commerce. Crossing a large vestibule, the visitor climbed a grand staircase to the main trading floor. At the building's dedication in 1885, one journalist reported: "One is struck with something akin to awe, transfixed as it were with the vastness, the splendid immensity of the most beautiful public interior thus far completed in this country."

FIGURE 26 shows the Board of Trade's large trading floor. The so-called Wheat Pit was "not a sunken amphitheater sort of place," as described by Robert Shackleton. Rather, it was a great open hall, with tall windows. "One sees masses of excited men," he wrote. "One hears a roar of sound, a rumbling shouting, strident boom of human voices, rising and falling, sinking in volume only to break

FIGURE 25. The Board of Trade Building, ca. 1905.

and out in rounds of speculative fever damaging to the very fabric of American society. It ruined farmers. It ruined merchants. It kited wealth to the top of the social pyramid. "All through the Northwest, . . . the set and whirl of that innermost Pit made itself felt; and it spread and spread and spread till grain in the elevators of Western Iowa moved and stirred and answered to its centripetal force, and men upon the streets of New York felt the mysterious tugging of its undertow engage their feet, embrace their bodies, overwhelm them, and carry them bewildered and unresisting back and downwards to the Pit itself."

The streets of downtown Chicago were organized in a rectilinear grid of some forty-two blocks. With streets meeting at right angles, the cornices of buildings, in one visitor's words, traced "geometry gone mad." Through the 1920s, building heights were limited by municipal ordinance; the city fathers were determined to prevent the shadowed "canyons" that had begun to plague Manhattan. Thus the Loop was a place of remarkable uniformity, with buildings upwards of twenty stories in height tightly packed together (see figures 7 and 21). "Unlike other cities," Robert Shackleton reported, "there are few landmarks noticeable in the business section." Certainly there was a lack of open squares with attention-getting monuments, but there was also "an absence of noticeable alternations of highness and lowness in buildings." "There is a sense of singular compactness and evenness in all the street scenes in the heart of the city," he wrote.

Viewed from above, a kind of sameness played out across the flat roofs of the city, each building with its chimney or smokestack, its water tank, its ventilators, and its skylights. But at street level, distinctiveness was clearly apparent as one walked from one specialty district to another. There was the jewelers' row, centered at Madison Street and Wabash Avenue, and the realtors'

into greater and more vociferous noise. And, intermittently, when the tumult and the shouting dies, one hears the staccato ticking of the rows of telegraph instruments off at one side." Frank Norris, of course, used the pit not to celebrate what was right about American capitalism in places such as Chicago, but to criticize what was wrong. It was, he wrote, "a great whirlpool . . . of roaring waters" that "spun and thundered, sucking in the life-tides of the city." As he saw it, wealth was siphoned in

FIGURE 26. The trading floor at the Board of Trade, 1908.

row, along Dearborn Street. The alleys offered some contrast, although to Shackleton they were "without picturesque appearance," meaning that they were mainly utilitarian. "That they are an aid in loading trucks, and that they uncomfortably break the level walking for those on sidewalks, is about all that can be said for them." Some things, such as the restaurants, could be encountered almost everywhere: "Wherever you look, in this central section you see some eating place," Shackleton wrote. "They are on corners and between blocks, they are on sidewalk level and upstairs and in basements: cafeterias, restaurants, waffle shops, with rivalry in not-distinguished names. There are the Universal, the Wonder . . . , the Red Star and the Puritan; there are the Pony and the Little Gem; one offers 'Quick Lunch for Bizzy Business Men: Eat it and Beat it'; numbers have but a single word over the doors, 'Eat.'"

TALL BUILDINGS

Before the arrival of the electric elevator, buildings in Chicago rarely rose above six stories, the level beyond which most people refused to climb by stair. The elevator, along with various other technological improvements, especially the use of iron and steel frame construction, made taller buildings not only possible but impelling. Previously, sole reliance on exterior walls of masonry, which tapered upward from bulky foundations, had also limited building heights. When masonry walls were more than fifteen or sixteen stories tall, they were so thick at ground level as to preclude retail shops, thus reducing rental income to the point of making development risky. Haltingly through the 1880s, Chicago architects and their clients embraced metal skeletal frames, initially only for interior building support, but ultimately for a building's entire weight load.

FIGURE 27. The Pullman Building, ca. 1900.

FIGURE 28. The Monadnock Building, ca. 1910.

Few of Chicago's new office buildings were as elegant at the Pullman Building (FIGURE 27), located on Michigan Avenue across from Grant Park. It was something of an ego trip for George Pullman, the successful capitalist, with its lavish cladding of brown brick and matching terra-cotta set above a base of rusticated stone. Placed at one corner was a decorative tower, itself an extravagance. Most of Chicago's new office buildings, however, were giant yet simple, plainly clad boxes, which totally filled the volume of space allowed above their allotted footprints. Wrote one disgruntled visitor, H. C. Chatfield-Taylor, "Blame not the architects whose task is to get the most rent per cubic foot with the least possible outlay, but rather the avaricious owners of real estate, and the supine aldermen whose baneful ordinances have permitted our cities to be distorted out of all architectural proportion."

The tallest commercial load-bearing masonry building ever constructed was the sixteen-story Monadnock Building on Dearborn Street (FIG-

FIGURE 29A. The Fisher Building, ca. 1920.

FIGURE 29B. The Commercial National Bank Building, ca. 1910.

URE 28), designed by the architectural firm of Holabird and Roche, and erected between 1891 and 1893. It was the largest office building in the world when completed. Initially it was criticized for its stark appearance, especially its lack of traditional decorative motif or styling. Its functional, stripped-down aesthetic anticipated early-twentieth-century modernism.

Supported by a skeletal frame of steel, the facade of the Fisher Building displayed Chicago's signature tripartite design for tall buildings—

base, shaft, and capital. To the eyes of pedestrians in the street, or as depicted in postcard views such as FIGURE 29A, these buildings appeared not only to be well-grounded, but to soar upward in logical visual termination. Skyrocketing property values in Chicago's downtown fostered more intensive land use through investor speculation in tall buildings. At the same time, telegraph and telephone communications enabled business managers to separate themselves from factory and warehouse floors in downtown locations close to

THE PEOPLES GAS BUILDING, CHICAGO

D. H. Burnham & Co., Architects

FIGURE 30. The Peoples Gas Building, ca. 1910.

the card, sent to a woman friend, he outlined his visit: "Chicago: Train, Streetcar, Great Northern Hotel, Marshall Fields, Vaudeville, Art Institute, Automobile, Gone."

The Peoples Gas Company supplied gas (obtained from coal and coke) for heating, cooking, and, initially, illumination. Pictured in FIGURE 30 is the company's giant office building, sheathed in white terra-cotta, one corner seemingly thrust up boldly into the sky, perhaps symbolic of corporate Chicago's assertiveness. As a government-regulated monopoly, in 1910 the company was delivering gas through some 3,100 miles of main buried beneath city streets, part of the underground infrastructure of the city, which, unlike the tower pictured here, was difficult to represent in postcard art. Chicago's other major utility, Commonwealth Edison, also erected a landmark office building in the Loop. However, few of the city's early office towers were put up by corporations. Most were built by developers on speculation. Such a building, nonetheless, might attract the business operatives of a single industry who preferred to be together not only for convenience, but for mutual support. For example, coal agents tended to locate in Chicago's Old Colony Building, whereas railroad ticket agents (and indeed the headquarters of several of the city's railroads) were concentrated mainly in the Railway Exchange Building.

With its leaded glass ceiling, marble columns, decorative light standards, benches, and mosaic tile floor, the atrium of the Peoples Gas Building spoke positively as a business address: an inside space that echoed the building's classically inspired exterior decor (FIGURE 31). Here was a place of refuge where people could arrange to meet, or where one could simply rest beyond the swirl of the city streets outside. Located here were the elevators that gave access to office floors above, as well as the stairs that gave access to shops that opened onto a mezzanine level. As Robert Shackle-

increasingly important banking, legal, accounting, and other professional services.

The tall office building symbolized not only power but also success, something that every individual could relate to. A young man visiting Chicago in 1907 scrawled across a view of the then-new Commercial National Bank the following words: "Will be president of a like institution some day" (FIGURE 29B). On the back of

FIGURE 31. Lobby of the Peoples Gas Building, ca. 1910.

ton described it, "The entrance-way opened into a great square-pillared Italian-like enclosed piazza, two stories high, all in white porcelain, and there was a glorious stair of white marble, and this costly interior court was surrounded by attractive interior shops, on two separate stories, here around the big central court, shops of hatters, opticians, tailors, manicures, shops for the sale of candy or cigars or flowers."

John S. Hawkinson and Company, in the Railway Exchange Building, sold ceramic tiles for mosaic floors, walls, and fireplaces. In the foreground of the postcard image in **FIGURE 32** is a demonstration tile floor, with cabinets on either side for storing stock. A table provides work space. The office opened out onto the building's mezzanine. This card, undoubtedly commissioned by Hawkinson as a means of advertising his business, offers a glimpse into how offices were or-

ganized and furnished at the time. Designed by Burnham and Company, which retained partial ownership, the building opened in 1904. It was essentially a giant cube with a hollowed-out square footprint above a two-story atrium by a large central light court. Rows of offices lined both sides of a central hallway on each upper floor. In Burnham-designed buildings, offices ranged from twenty to twenty-eight feet in depth, and were usually divided into two sections. Floor space near the windows was usually partitioned off as a private area for the business manager; the remainder, near the outer door, was reserved for public entry. There, in the "borrowed light" that filtered through glazed translucent wall panels, stenographers and other support staff worked. Air circulated through door transoms.

Nowhere were Chicago's tall buildings more impressive than along Michigan Avenue at Grant

JOHN S. HAWKINSON CO., 243 RAILWAY EXCHANGE BLDG., CHICAGO, ILL.

FIGURE 32. Office of the John S. Hawkinson Company in the Railway Exchange Building, ca. 1910.

Park. Here was Chicago's "front door," the avenue that put the city's best face forward. Buildings formed a cliff-like "wall," providing Grant Park on the right with a sharp visual edge. The view in FIGURE 33 is looking north, past prominent landmark buildings: the mansard-roofed Blackstone Hotel, the Harvester Building, the Congress Hotel, the Auditorium Building, the McCormick Building, the Railway Exchange Building, the Peoples Gas Building. A smorgasbord of architectural styles were adapted to these tall buildings: French Second Empire, Venetian Gothic, Romanesque Revival, Classical Revival. Structurally dominant, however, was the tripartite skyscraper of the "Chicago School." Visitors were primed to be impressed. As one tourist brochure read: "On one side towering skyscrapers that stretch blocks and blocks north and south; on the other, the expanse

of Lake Michigan which gives the glamour and color and bigness to this enchanted highway."

Precedent was set for preserving the lakefront for recreational use in 1835, when the federal government relinquished its military reservation south of the river to the commissioners of the Illinois and Michigan Canal, designating it as "A Common to Remain Forever Open, Clear and Free of any Buildings, or other Obstruction Whatever." For that intent to be sustained, however, decades of litigation were required, much of it led by Aaron Montgomery Ward, founder of the mail-order house that bore his name, who was motivated partly by the desire to preserve the view from his office window. (The tower of the Montgomery Ward Building is just visible in the far distance in this view.) The park, named in 1901 to honor Ulysses S. Grant, was landscaped follow-

FIGURE 33. A view north along Michigan Avenue at Grant Park, ca. 1920.

ing classically inspired principles borrowed from Versailles, and thus it also echoed the layout of the World's Columbian Exposition. The tracks of the Illinois Central Railroad are visible off to the right. As Julian Street observed, "trains ... continue to puff, importantly, along the lake front, their locomotives issuing great clouds of steam and smoke, which are snatched by the lake wind, and hurled like giant snowballs—dirty snowballs, full of cinders—at the imperturbable stone front of Michigan Avenue."

With building height restrictions removed, Chicago developers began to copy the aesthetics of New York City skyscrapers. Chicago's zoning regulations of 1923, like New York's earlier zoning law, encouraged the use of building setbacks. The skyscraper pictured in FIGURE 34 was originally called the Jewelers' Building, because of its location at the center of the city's "Jewelers' Row." The name was changed when the Pure Oil Company became the principal tenant in 1926. Pure

Oil, which began as a gas utility in Ohio, turned to refining and marketing gasoline when wells in its West Virginia gas fields also started producing petroleum. The company built a large refinery south of Chicago along the Des Plaines River, and quickly came to supply the gas stations of a broad midwestern market.

New York–styled skyscrapers with towers perched on towers characterized tall-building construction in Chicago in the 1920s. FIGURE 35A shows a cluster of such buildings facing the Chicago River. Depicted at the center is the London Guarantee and Accident Building, completed just before the city's height restrictions were liberalized. Thus the neo-Greco/neo-Roman structure is topped with a classical cupola rather than a soaring tower extension. Later buildings did soar through staged setbacks, including the Mather Tower, seen here immediately behind the London Guarantee and Accident Building, and both the Carbide and Carbon Building and the 333

FIGURE 34. The Pure Oil Building, ca. 1930.

FIGURE 35A. Michigan Avenue at Wacker Drive, 1933.

North Michigan Avenue Building to the left. Visitor Henry Justin Smith described the distinctive silhouette that Chicago's new skyline presented: "There is no other urban sky-line quite like it in the world. Its perspective to north or south is longer than a stranger anticipates. Its upper lines are as jagged as a bolt of lightning. Here a tower shoots aloft; there a roof sinks to the level of pre-sky-scraper days."

The nearby Michigan Avenue Bridge was a massive double-decked, double-leafed bascule structure that "rose into the air like an alligator's jaws when ships whistled," in the words of Lloyd Lewis. Opened in 1920, it allowed for the extension of Michigan Avenue north of the river. FIGURE 35B shows the pedestrian approach from the north. Sculptures offer an allegorical reference to the city's historic past, Fort Dearborn having been located close to the bridge crossing.

The Board of Trade Building rose from street level through a series of setbacks that culminated with a shaft seemingly thrust upward through

FIGURE 35B. The north approach to the Michigan Avenue Bridge over the Chicago River, ca. 1925.

FIGURE 36. The new Chicago Board of Trade Building, ca. 1935.

the structure's center. Opened in 1930, the building was ornamented in Art Deco style by the long-established Chicago architectural firm of Holabird and Root, whose founders helped pioneer steel frame construction. The caption on the postcard in FIGURE 36 reads: "A forty-four story building stands majestically at the head of La Salle Street, the center of Chicago's financial district. The trading floor is more modern and perfect in its mechanical facilities than any other exchange in the world. Topped by a statue of Ceres, 'God-

dess of Wheat.'" Graham Hutton, author of the widely read *Midwest at Noon*, wrote: "Go to the remarkable observatory . . . above the 'wheat pit,' and walk all round looking out for miles across railyards, stockyards, great public buildings, hotels, skyscrapers, each commercial building with its water tank atop, and as far as you can see in all directions but one—eastward where the lake runs straight north and south—there are the evidences of hectic activity: producing, transforming, packing, merchandising, printing, transporting,

FIGURE 37. The Prudential Building along Michigan Avenue viewed from the Chicago Institute of Art, 1958.

financing, selling, advertising, bustling, jostling, hurrying." In this postcard image, LaSalle Street is empty. Were the evidences of a chaotic mad dash expunged—the picture sanitized to enhance the clean modernity of the new building? Or was the photo taken on a Sunday, or on a holiday? One suspects it was a Sunday.

The Depression of the 1930s and then World War II kept skyscraper construction in Chicago at a standstill. The Prudential Building (**FIGURE 37**), designed by Sigurd Naess and Charles F. Murphy, was completed in 1955, becoming the city's tallest structure at 600 feet, and also the first to be built with "air rights," in this case over the lakefront yards of the Illinois Central Railroad. It anticipated still another departure in Chicago tall-building architecture: a modernism that fully favored plainness in decor, the use of simple geometric massing, and new cladding materials, especially metal

and glass. But the Prudential Building was not the minimalist statement that modern architects such as Ludwig Mies van der Rohe would later add to the Chicago skyline, thus fostering a second "Chicago School," a design enthusiasm that local firms such as Skidmore, Owings and Merrill (SOM) successfully promoted worldwide in ensuing decades.

Only one building, the pavilion of the Chicago Institute of Art, shown on the right, proved a permanent intrusion into Grant Park. It dated from the World's Columbian Exposition of 1893; the fair's commissioners and the commissioners of the South Park District had agreed to share the construction costs, with the structure to be used temporarily for the fair's academic congresses. The building was massed and decorated in the Italian Renaissance style, a motif that was thought to symbolize the humanistic ideals of the Renaissance and the Enlightenment. Visitors entered from Michigan Avenue, climbing up broad steps past two giant lions on either side. The Art Institute had long benefited from elite patronage, proof that capitalist Chicago had come of age culturally.

Marina City (FIGURE 38) broke early with modernism's strict rectangular regularity. The architect, Bertrand Goldberg, thus anticipated the eclectic styling of the so-called postmodern age by more than a decade. Marina City also pioneered the "city-within-a-city" concept, its two towers being part of a five-building complex intended for work, residency, and leisure activities: a place that would be used twenty-four hours a day. The towers, the tallest yet to be built of steel-reinforced concrete, were each organized around a cylindrical utility core using the then-novel "slip-form" construction technique. The floors were extended, one above another, outward from each completed core; each building contained 450 pie-shaped apartments in 40 stories located above a 20-story parking deck. Pundits quickly likened the two towers to giant corncobs: a symbolic expression, perhaps, of Chicago's roots in Downstate Illinois cornfields.

As skyscrapers appeared along North Michigan Avenue, a new downtown was born. Initially called the "Boul Mich," after the Parisian boulevard with that nickname, but later renamed the "Magnificent Mile," Michigan Avenue north of the river was actually a remake of lowly Pine Street, a narrow thoroughfare lined with aging warehouses and mansions. During the economic boom of the 1920s, the raised and widened avenue came to sport fashionable shops, luxury hotels, and prestigious office buildings where most of the city's advertising agencies clustered. In the nighttime view in FIGURE 39, the Wrigley Building is pictured on the left, and the Tribune Tower on the right, beyond which can be seen the dome of the Medinah Club, the roof of the Allerton Hotel, and the

FIGURE 38. The Marina City Towers viewed from State Street, 1964.

Palmolive Building, with its beacon boldly dubbed in. Barely visible in the middle distance is the historic water tower that survived the 1871 fire. Chicago's "Latin Quarter," which some Chicagoans called "Towertown," centered on streets west of that landmark.

The Wrigley Building, designed for chewing gum king William Wrigley by Charles Beerman of Graham, Anderson and Probst (a firm descended from Daniel Burnham and Company), was in fact

FIGURE 39. A view of North Michigan Avenue north from the Chicago River, ca. 1935.

international competition to design "the world's most beautiful building" to honor as well as house the "world's greatest newspaper," the *Chicago Tribune*, on its seventy-fifth anniversary. Designed in Gothic Revival style, the cathedral-like gray limestone-clad building was terminated at the top with a crown. The building did not live up to expectations as a design precedent, but several of the losing entries, by architects such as Eliel Saarinen, Walter Gropius, and Adolf Loos, proved highly influential in subsequent skyscraper design both in Chicago and across the globe.

The limestone-clad, Art Deco–styled Palmolive Building, designed by Holabird and Root, rose thirty-seven stories through a series of setbacks. The building's beacon, originally named in honor of Charles Lindbergh, rotated twice a minute, the world's most powerful at 2 billion candlepower. According to a state guidebook, "At an altitude of 45,000 feet it can be seen 500 miles; the average visibility is 250 miles. Newspapers have been read by its light in planes 27 miles away." The yellow sandstone water tower, opened just two years before the 1871 fire, contained a 138-foot-tall standpipe that stabilized water pressure across the northern part of the city, water being drawn from the lake and distributed from a pumping station located across Michigan Avenue.

HOTELS

Hotel postcards were common, as Americans routinely dashed off messages to friends and family while traveling. After all, hotel advertising cards were free. The card in FIGURE 40 is from the Palmer House, long recognized as the city's leading hostelry. The handwritten message reads: "Arrived here at 5 o'clock a.m. Will leave for Goldfield at 11:45 a.m. With love to all. Your father." The rebuilding of Chicago's downtown immediately after the 1871 fire added some 5,000 hotel rooms. Potter Palmer and his architect, John Van Osdel, toured

two buildings, the larger of which was topped by a tall tower. Perhaps it was the dazzling nighttime effects of the 1893 "White City" that inspired Beerman's use of sparkling terra-cotta. It certainly shown brilliantly when floodlit after dark, as this postcard depiction suggests. Six shades of tile were specified, ranging from creamy white at the bottom to blue-white at the top, in order to sustain an even brightness as people looked up from street level. The Tribune Tower resulted from an

Chicago
Palmer House on State St.

Hazen 3/29-07

arrived here at 5° K'an will leave for Goldfield at 11 4/5 a.m. heir love to all your Fathe m. m.

FIGURE 40. Advertising postcard for the Palmer House Hotel, ca. 1900.

Europe to look at grand hotels in anticipation of rebuilding the Palmer House; the trip produced the French Renaissance–styled building pictured here. A new Palmer House, built in the 1920s, carried on the hotel's reputation as the city's premier hostelry. It was "the most monstrous of all the hotels I've seen," wrote a French visitor to the city in the 1930s. "Bar, cafeteria, lunchroom, blue room, red room, Victorian room, gypsy orchestra, Mexican orchestra, flowers, candy, all sorts of stores, travel offices, airlines—it's a whole town with its residential neighborhoods, its quiet avenues, and its noisy commercial downtown."

Completed in 1892, the Auditorium Building (FIGURE 41) was intended as a cultural center for the city, and indeed it remained so for well over half a century, an important symbol of Chicago's civic progress. "This is one of the finest theaters in the world, noted for the frequent display and

brilliance of its assemblages," championed Rand McNally's *Bird's-Eye Views and Guide to Chicago*, It seated close to 6,000 people and hosted events from grand opera to national political conventions. Besides its auditorium, the building contained a 400-room hotel, which, along with the Palmer House, attracted society's elite. Several floors were given over to offices. An observation platform, some 240 feet above Michigan Avenue, topped the prominent tower. Designed in Romanesque Revival style, the Auditorium Building launched the international reputations of two Chicago architects, Dankmar Adler and Louis H. Sullivan. Its hotel anchored what became a Michigan Avenue "hotel row" with the Stratford, Congress, Blackstone, and other hostelries. After World War II, the building housed Chicago's Roosevelt University.

FIGURE 42 shows the Hotel Sherman in 1934. Like the Palmer House, the well-respected Sher-

FIGURE 41. The Auditorium Building, ca. 1920.

FIGURE 42. Advertising postcard for the Hotel Sherman, 1934.

FIGURE 43. Lobby of the Hotel LaSalle, ca. 1915.

man House withstood the competition of the mammoth new hotels built in downtown Chicago early in the twentieth century, among them the 1909 Hotel LaSalle, with 1,000 rooms; the 1925 Morrison Hotel, with 2,000 rooms; and the largest of them all, and in fact the largest hotel in the world when it was completed, the 1927 Hotel Stevens, with 3,000 rooms. They did so, of course, by becoming mammoth themselves. In the case of the new Hotel Sherman, an attached parking garage helped attract the increasing number of visitors to Chicago who were arriving by automobile. This postcard clearly shows how the hotel was enlarged over time, with the garage being part of a late-1920s addition. Each of the city's grand hotels offered guest rooms with private toilet and bath facilities as well as an assortment of suites, including bridal suites, to suit the well-to-do. Chi-

cago's large hotels, it might be said, both reflected and celebrated capitalist values that were fully bourgeois in nature.

In Chicago, as in other American cities, hotels offered more than just lodging. They were intended to be, and indeed did function like, private clubs, complete with smoking, reading, music, and reception rooms. Hotels originally catered mainly to men; women were often confined to separate "family" entrances, and if they were unaccompanied by a male companion, they were restricted from many of the hotel's public spaces. Those spaces, such as the Hotel LaSalle's lobby and registration desk (**FIGURE 43**), were lavishly appointed, in replication, as foreign visitors to the city especially liked to note, of Europe's aristocratic palaces. Wrote Englishman Robert Shackleton: "You enter another hotel and find a long passageway, where

FIGURE 44. Electric sign, Grant Park, 1915.

"Chicago is the meeting place of the world," boasted the editors of the *Rand McNally Guide to Chicago and Environs*. "Situated in the center of a population of 60,000,000 people within a night's ride, Chicago has ample provision for the hundreds of thousands of visitors who flock to the city annually. Conventions alone bring more than 600,000 strangers into the city yearly and they are not without a place to lay their heads. Chicago's normal hotel capacity is in excess of 100,000 rooms per day." Temporary signs to greet convention guests were regularly erected in Grant Park. **FIGURE 44** shows the sign that welcomed the Knights Templar to the organization's thirty-first annual convention in 1915. Chicago did not have a "Great White Way" like New York City's Broadway. In Chicago, electric-sign spectaculars such as this one were dispersed across downtown. Here, however, was a sign to brag about, as the accompanying card asserts: "Highest Spectacular Electric Sign in the World. . . . Height 133 Feet."

LAKE AND RIVER

In the twentieth century, Chicago was generally thought of as facing across Grant Park toward Lake Michigan. **FIGURE 45** features a nighttime view of the Buckingham Fountain, a Grant Park centerpiece. Designed by Edward H. Bennett, co-author with Daniel Burnham of the 1909 *Plan of Chicago*, the fountain (with seahorse sculptures by Marcel Loyau), shot a central column of water some 100 feet into the air. "At night, hidden lights of 45 million candlepower concentrate a blaze of color, constantly shifting in pattern, on the cascades of spray," wrote the authors of a state guidebook. Grant Park figured prominently in Chicago's iconography. In no other American city was water so easily accessible. The Lake Front Ordinance of 1919 redefined the city's commitment to lakefront improvement. Soon a parkway extended many of Grant Park's amenities both north and south

everybody meets everybody, a place full of animation. And there is a gorgeous Pompeian room, with pillars and pilasters of black and white, and wall panels of brilliant Pompeian red, and there are a fountain and an orchestra playing beside a sunken pool. And one may go into an English room, an Elizabethan room with dark oak and high ceiling, with windows of leaded glass, a room of wonderful effectiveness, in its subdued lights and its grave beauty."

FIGURE 45. Buckingham Fountain, Grant Park, ca. 1915.

along some fifteen miles of lakeshore. The drive up from the south along the lake after dark was "astoundingly splendid," wrote two visitors from the Soviet Union. "To the right was blackness. . . . On the left rows of skyscrapers stretched for several miles. . . . The lights of the upper stories of the skyscrapers mingled with the stars."

Soldier Field (**FIGURE 46**), named in honor of the servicemen killed in World War I, was built immediately south of Grant Park. Holabird and Roche won the competition to design the U-shaped amphitheater, the exterior ornamentation for which they modeled after the Parthenon. The structure, however, was perhaps more reminiscent of the Roman Coliseum, a symbol of public splendor. Spectators seated high up in the stadium's lakeside stands enjoyed an extraordinary view of the city's skyline. After World War II, the Chicago Bears, the professional football team that had moved up to

the city from Decatur, regularly played there. The stadium also hosted events such as religious services, convention gatherings, track meets, and prize fights. The caption on this postcard reads in part: "One of the largest Stadiums in the world, having seating capacity of over 122,000." In sports as in all things, bigness was something to celebrate.

Also visible in this image, beyond the stadium, is the Field Museum of Natural History, endowed by the department store magnate Marshall Field. "A great flight of steps leads to the majestic pedimented portico, two rows of columns in depth," wrote the author of a state historical guide. "This is flanked by long wings, four stories high, that are decorated with Ionic colonnades ending in transverse halls." In addition to its geology, zoology, and botany collections, the museum was noted for its large holding of Native American items. "The first floor has seven halls devoted to

FIGURE 46. Soldier Field, ca. 1930.

Indians of the Americas, offering a remarkable comprehensive display of the artifacts and habiliments of a vast population that once covered the continent." For most Chicagoans, and Illinoisans generally, "Native America" was something confined mainly to museums.

The waterfronts of American cities were typically dominated by commercial and industrial activity. That was definitely true of the Chicago River, the city's only harbor before Navy Pier was built, and before the Lake Calumet basin was improved for shipping. Commonly pictured in postcard art was the Rush Street swing bridge, which, before the extension of Michigan Avenue northward, was the principal river crossing between the city's north and south sides (see figure 3). Lined with grain elevators, warehouses, and factories, including the McCormick Implement Works, this stretch of river, just west of Lake Michigan, appeared to many commentators to be the city's

true heart and soul. On the one hand, it was, as a resident noted, the most forbidding part of the city, a "region of dilapidated buildings and ill-paved streets." On the other hand, he continued, "Yet this rookery is the part of our city best entitled to be qualified as old, for here is the seat of a history vying in age with almost any in the land. Here, too, is the main reach of the river whence sprang the city's greatness and from which it takes its name." He added: "I seldom cross the Rush Street Bridge afoot without stopping to gaze at this alluring river, and to dream of the changes time's magic has wrought."

On the river's south branch, out beyond Bridgeport, the vibrant Irish neighborhood where the very first bridge across the river had been built, lay the city's lumber district, each of its numerous boat slips backed by a large lumberyard (FIGURE 47). Logs and rough-hewn timber from the forests of the upper Great Lakes accumulated here

Lumber District, Chicago, Ill.

FIGURE 47. Chicago's lumber district along the South Branch of the Chicago River, ca. 1915.

to be milled. In 1923, Chicago received, mainly by water, some 3.5 billion board feet of lumber and shipped out, mainly by rail, about two-thirds of it.

Chicago was much more than a lumber port. As the giant grain elevators along the Chicago River suggest (see figure 3), the city was a major grain handler. It was also a major wholesaling center, with a "water carrying trade" that was "comparable to that of the greatest ocean ports of the country, New York and Boston, and exceeds that of Philadelphia, New Orleans, Baltimore and San Francisco," heralded one city guide. Observed journalist George Engelhardt: "The receipts by water . . . embrace, besides large quantities of staple commodities—groceries, canned goods, hardware, dry goods, etc.—a vast tonnage of green fruits, sugar, salt, hides and leather, paper, cement and plaster, coal and iron ore, much

of it the product of lake tributaries of the city, and sixty percent of the incoming lumber; while the shipments include over half of the vast quantity of grain handled here." And all of this was accomplished despite the river's narrow confines, which made for "one of the most inconvenient and restricted harbors in the world." Shipping in and out of Chicago was seasonal, with lake navigation necessarily curtailed from December through February.

Numerous excursion steamers linked Chicago with Milwaukee to the north, and with various resort towns across the lake in Michigan. Vacation-oriented cruise ships also connected the city with more distant places, including Detroit, Cleveland, and Buffalo. Most popular, however, were the pleasure boats that offered day trips. Carl Sandburg wrote:

STEAMSHIP "CHRISTOPHER COLUMBUS" IN CHICAGO RIVER

FIGURE 48. The cruise ship *Christopher Columbus*, ca. 1915.

Sunday night and the park policemen tell
    each other it is dark as a stack of black cats
    on Lake Michigan.
A big picnic boat comes home to Chicago from
    the peach farms of Saugatuck.

. . . .

Over the hoarse crunch of waves . . . comes. . .
    the rhythmic oompa of the brasses playing a
    Polish folk-song for the homecomers.

On July 25, 1915, disaster struck the passenger ship *Eastland*. Crowded with more than 2,000 employees and guests of the Chicago-based Western Electric Company, the maker of telephone equipment for the giant Bell System, the vessel turned over at wharf-side. A total of 812 people drowned, including twenty-two entire families. Pictured in **FIGURE 48** is another cruise ship, the *Christopher Columbus*, with its distinctive "whale-back" look.

Aging warehouses and factory buildings, stacks of lumber, piles of coal, and dust-laden grain elevators posed a constant fire threat. In 1871, a large warehouse fire along the river's south branch so depleted the city's water reservoirs that when Mrs. O'Leary's proverbial cow kicked over the proverbial stable lantern (a story long since discredited), the city's fire department was unable to contain the windblown flames. The fire leapt the river, swept across downtown, and crossed the river once again to spend itself just north of the city's waterworks. At least 300 people lost their lives, and 18,000 buildings across nearly four square miles of the city were destroyed; approximately 30 percent of the total property value in the city was wiped out. As in every American city, fires in large buildings frequently resulted in great loss of life; the 1903 fire in Chicago's Iroquois Theater, for example, killed some 800 people. But when postcards depicted fire, they did so in ways that were reassuring. In **FIGURE 49**, a municipal

FIGURE 49. A fireboat on the Chicago River, ca. 1910.

fireboat is depicted as if in action, with much of the illustration dubbed in.

WHOLESALING

By 1920, warehousing and light industry had came to dominate the Chicago River's margins except where railroad tracks took precedence. George Engelhardt described the Chicago River as "a narrow riband of inky current, but deep and navigable, and extensively navigated too; lined on both sides with warehouses and factories, railroad yards and sidings, immense grain elevators and coal hoists, and spanned with fifty bridges or more in its brief course of ten or twelve miles." Although the river figured prominently in people's mental maps of the city, it and its margins were rarely sought out as places to linger; there were better locales in which to spend time. For example, the personal note written on the back of the postcard in FIGURE 50 reads: "I am down at the beach watching the children playing in the lovely sand. Lake Michigan is beautiful today." Much of the city's warehousing was sited along the river. Chicago was very much a "gateway city." Not only were grain, livestock, lumber, and other commodities assembled there for shipment, but a wide range of manufactured goods were distributed from Chicago across a vast hinterland, a trade territory skewed westward along the railroads.

By 1920, motorized traffic congestion in the Loop had become a serious problem. Depicted in FIGURE 51 is an idealized view of what city planners anticipated once the old warehouses and factories along the Chicago River were removed and the waterfront was improved as a motorway. Charles H. Wacker, chairman of the Chicago Plan Commission, oversaw construction of the double-decked "boulevard," the top level of which was intended

FIGURE 50. The Chicago River west from the Wrigley Building, ca. 1920.

FIGURE 51. Plan for Wacker Drive, Chicago Plan Commission, 1920.

FIGURE 52A. The Merchandise Mart, ca. 1940.

for automobiles and the lower for delivery trucks. Its first phase, completed in 1926, required the condemnation and purchase of more than 3,000 properties. The project was intended not only to make the Loop more convenient to motorists and truckers but also to stabilize the river's embankments and improve their appearance. In addition, it was intended to stimulate land development. "Below is a subterranean passage filled with noisy trucks," wrote the authors of *All about Chicago*. "The upper level, thronged with hurrying motors, is waiting for its quota of skyscrapers which will one day present a facade rivaling the great panorama of buildings on Michigan Avenue."

Improved sanitation and flood control, although less visible, was no less important. Completion of the Sanitary and Ship Canal, connecting with the Illinois River some twenty-eight miles southwest at Lockport in 1900, and the installation of giant pumps at Bridgeport had reversed the river's flow. The Chicago River had become an outlet for the lake, instead of the lake remaining an outlet for the river. "It carries away the sewage, offers a water-way for boats, and at the same time is so constructed, with water power and power stations, as to generate for the city an enormous supply of electricity," wrote Robert Shackleton. The digging of the Sanitary and Ship Canal, as well the digging of the Cal-Sag Channel decades later along the city's southernmost boundary, generated much of the fill used in extending Chicago's lakeshore parkland out into Lake Michigan.

Many of the city's wholesalers removed to one or another giant office block well away from the river, such as the Furniture Mart or the Merchandise Mart, the latter of which is pictured in FIGURE 52A. The caption on this postcard reads: "World's largest building, on North Bank Drive and Wells St. 'A wholesale city under one roof.' It houses several hundred wholesale merchandise concerns representing Chicago, the Great Central Market." With some 4 million square feet of floor

1942. ". Some Post Office." Chicago. NEW CHICAGO POST OFFICE NOW BEING ERECTED N93
22,000 persons work here at all shifts. Built 1933. Chicago
(Biggest P.O. in the World.) new P.O.

(Railroad mail trains Enter in the Basement.) Subway.)

FIGURE 52B. The new Chicago Post Office, 1934..

space, the building was constructed over air rights above the Chicago and Northwestern Railroad. The use of air rights in and around the city's downtown came to play a very important role in real estate development. Another huge building completed along the Chicago River was the new post office, the largest postal facility in the world when it was completed in the 1930s. The collector of the unsent postcard shown in FIGURE 52B recorded the building's importance on the face: "20,000 people work here.... Biggest P.O. in the World."

THE PRODUCE MARKET

Chicago's produce market was initially centered on Water Street immediately south of the Chicago River's main stem, ultimately to extend westward across the river's south branch, mainly along Randolph Street. There, just as at the Board of Trade and at the mammoth grain elevators along the

river, Chicago's connection to and reliance upon its agricultural hinterland was fully obvious. The postcard in FIGURE 53 shows Haymarket Square, a widened section of Randolph Street, where, on the evening of May 4, 1886, a bomb tossed at a labor rally killed eight policemen and wounded sixty others. Chicago had become the focus of a nationwide drive to establish the eight-hour workday. The violence followed days of meetings and parades spearheaded by German American trade unionists that had followed from a general strike held on the first of May, the "May Day" that inspired the labor movement worldwide. Four "conspirators" were sentenced to death in what today is generally viewed as one of the worst miscarriages of justice in American history, a trial that crystalized many of the social antagonisms that dominated American politics for decades thereafter. American society was rapidly urbanizing, and

Haymarket Square, Chicago.
Produce Market Scene of Anarchist riot in 1888.

FIGURE 53. Haymarket Square, West Randolph Street, ca. 1905.

dividing not only along class lines, but in ways that pitted the native-born against the foreign-born. So defining a moment was the Haymarket Affair that postcard publishers could not ignore it. This card's subtitle shared the establishment view at the time, which failed to see the episode as largely provoked by police action: "Produce Market Scene of Anarchist Riot," it reads.

The near-chaos of the city's bustling produce market offered a spectacle that lent itself to post-card depiction (**FIGURE 54**). There one could see every variety of farm product, including exotic foods from faraway climes: "magnificent pine-apples, fourteen days from Honolulu, oranges from California and Florida, and bananas from Central America, with apples from Washington, Oregon and Michigan, and peaches and grapes from everywhere," one visitor wrote. Excitement lay in the overcrowding. "The sidewalks are filled

so completely with boxes, crates, barrels and baskets that passers must go in single file and crowd in between the barrels to permit the passage of persons going in an opposite direction," he continued. Perhaps it was novelist Frank Norris who said it best. To him, South Water Street was "a jam of delivery wagons and market carts backed to the curbs, leaving only a tortuous path between the endless files of horses, suggestive of an actual barrack of cavalry. Provisions, market produce, 'garden truck' and fruits, in an infinite welter of crates and baskets, boxes, and sacks, crowded the sidewalks. The gutter was choked with an over-flow of refuse cabbage leaves, soft oranges, decaying beet tops. The air was thick with the heavy smell of vegetation. . . . Food mingled with the mud of the highway." The streets of the produce market stood in sharp contrast to State, LaSalle, and other downtown arteries that were noted

FIGURE 54. Produce market, South Water Street, ca. 1905.

for their decorum and neatness. On those streets, Chicago was defined more at the scale of the large corporation. But along South Water Street, and along Randolph Street as well, it was still a world of small capitalists: the vendor, the teamster, the storekeeper, the artisan.

Through the early period of the postcard's popularity, the horse rather than the internal combustion engine was king. Yet relatively few view cards of the early twentieth century featured horses. It was better, certainly for sales, if the images represented modernity, and hence newness, rather than things passé; thus cars and trucks were favored over carriages and wagons. Many an early postcard view was doctored: horses and wagons were blotted out, and cars and trucks, along with modern street lights and other evidence of "progress," were dubbed in. Indeed, horses ultimately gave way to motor vehicles in Chicago's pro-

duce market, but not until well after World War I. "Backed up to [the sidewalks there] are teams as thick as they can stand . . . receiving or delivering purchases." **FIGURE 55A** shows teamsters at a fountain sharing water with their horses, a level of intimacy between man and beast rarely pictured. Beer and hard liquor, of course, were the workingman's release from the drudgery of the market, warehouse, and factory. Many a factory gate opened directly onto a street lined with taverns. Pictured in **FIGURE 55B** is "Whiskey Row" near the Union Stock Yards.

As South Water Street gave way to Wacker Drive, much of its market function was transferred to a modern market to the west on Fifteenth Street, which was oriented to railroad sidings and fully convenient for trucks as well. The caption on the postcard in **FIGURE 56** reads: "View looking west along 15th Street from Morgan St.,

shows Chicago's principal produce market . Over 80,000 carloads of fruits and vegetable come into the market by rail and truck yearly. It is an important factor in contributing to Chicago's fame as the great central market." Trucks were to be preferred to horse-drawn wagons for many reasons, not the least of which was health and sanitation. The motor age largely brought an end to dung and urine in the streets, covered, at least in the summer months, with buzzing flies. Chicago was now a much cleaner place, or so most people thought, despite the hydrocarbons that internal combustion engines released into the air.

THE STOCKYARDS

"Packingtown" provided meat not only to Chicago and Illinois beyond the metropolis but nationwide as well (FIGURE 57). In contrast to the produce market, work in and around the stockyards was organized at the scale of the large factory:

FIGURE 55A. Teamsters, South Water Street, ca. 1905.

FIGURE 55B. "Whiskey Row."

FIGURE 56. West Fifteenth Street, ca. 1935.

FIGURE 57. The Union Stock Yards, ca. 1935.

FIGURE 58A. The Beef Dressing Department, Swift and Company, ca. 1915.

using not assembly lines, as in Chicago's implement plants, for example, but dis-assembly lines for the slaughter and carving up of hogs, sheep, and beef cattle (**FIGURE 58A**). Opened in 1865, the Union Stock Yards quickly became an important tourist destination. By 1900, the facility covered 475 acres and contained some 13,000 animal pens, several banks, a hotel, an amphitheater, 15 miles of sewer, 25 miles of street, 90 miles of water main, and more than 100 miles of railroad track. Some 25,000 workers were employed there, most of them immigrants recently arrived in the United States. It was packinghouse workers who had swelled the ranks of organized labor in 1886 and appeared so threatening to business leaders. The stock pens were interesting in and of themselves. As a city guide described, "Cattlemen from the plains, buyers and sellers are coming and going on foot and on horseback; at the side of each pen,

on top of the stout surrounding fence, is a narrow pathway where others who wish to buy or sell or simply look may inspect the animals from above at close range; here will be seen sheep, there hogs, then perhaps a bunch of calves, followed by pen after pen of fine steers from Kansas, Dakota and all over the western plains."

The Union Stock Yards were home to more than forty packing plants, prime among them the facilities of two industry giants: Swift and Company and Armour and Company. In 1929, animals arrived from twenty-seven states, including some 6.9 million hogs, 4.4 million sheep, and 1.7 million cattle. Approximately one-third of the animals were sent to feeder lots and packing plants farther east. The remainder were slaughtered, with the meat packed in tins to be boxed for shipment, or chilled for shipment in refrigerator cars. Large quantities of hide, hair, and wool were produced

FIGURE 58B. The Canned Foods Department, Armour and Company, ca. 1915.

as well, and Chicago packers turned discarded animal parts into glue, fertilizer, glycerin, ammonia, feed for livestock, pharmaceuticals, oil, fat, and soap. Upton Sinclair's revealing novel *The Jungle* (1906), which exposed sanitation and other problems at the Union Stock Yards, led Congress to pass the Meat Inspection Act.

What visitors remembered most vividly about the stockyard was inevitably the killing floors. "With varying degrees of shock," Henry Justin Smith wrote, "spectators, celebrated or unimportant, stand on visitors' platforms and watch the stunning of muscular steers or, in a grisly twilight, the slaughter of hogs amid steam, blood, and outcries." Observed Julian Street: "The progress of the pig is swift—if the transition from pig to pork may be termed 'progress.' The carcass travels presently through boiling water, and emerges pink and clean. And as it goes along upon its trolley, it passes one man after another, each with an active knife, until, thirty minutes later, where it has undergone the government inspection, it is headless and in halves—mere meat, which looks as though it never could have been alive."

Visitors avidly sought to be "behind the scenes" in the "back regions" of industrial Chicago. Nowhere were "work displays" more sought out than at the Union Stock Yards. "To watch an animal from the pen to the tin is an extraordinary experience," wrote one Chicago visitor. Nonetheless, it was what it was, he implied. "You see it killed; it falls; a conveyor carries it away. It is flayed while you wait. . . . you see the meat shredded; in another room the manicured girls are filling the shreds into tins, and the tin is closed and labeled. The thing that astounds is the quiet officialdom of this murder." **FIGURE 58B** shows the Canned Foods Department at Armour and Company.

BIRD'S-EYE VIEW BUSINESS DISTRICT OF CHICAGO
New Passenger Terminal, Chicago and North Western Ry., in foreground

FIGURE 59. The Chicago and Northwestern railroad station, ca. 1920.

RAILROADS AND FACTORIES

As Carl Sandburg put it, Chicago was a "Player with Railroads." Chicago, and to a lesser extent St. Louis, made Illinois the hub of the nation's railroad system. In 1939, thirty-three long-distance railroads served Chicago, whereas twenty-three served St. Louis. Consequently, Illinois had more railway mileage than any other state except Texas. And yet, Chicago's railroad infrastructure was poorly coordinated. Trains originated and terminated in the city but did not pass through. Passengers arriving in the city from the east who wanted to continue west were forced not only to change trains, but in most instances to change stations as well. On the other hand, freight did move through the city in freight cars. But cars were slow in being shunted from one line to another through the maze of nearly 100 classification yards.

FIGURE 59 shows the terminal of the Chicago and Northwestern Railroad, whose tracks connected Chicago with Minneapolis–St. Paul and Omaha, among other cities. The line's commuter trains also terminated here. Opened in 1911, the depot, located at West Madison and North Canal Streets, featured a large three-story waiting room, marble-walled and marble-pillared, trimmed in bronze. The rail yard that stretched north behind the station was described by Frank Norris in *The Pit* through the eyes of the novel's heroine, who is standing on a bridge. "Down below there, rectilinear, scientifically paralleled and squared, the Yard disclosed itself. A system of gray rails beyond words complicated, opened out, and spread immeasurably. Switches, semaphores, and signal towers stood here and there. A dozen trains, freight and passenger, puffed and steamed, waiting the word to depart. Detached engines hurried in and out of

104620

FIGURE 60. The concourse at Union Station, 1925.

sheds and round-houses, seeking their trains, or bunted the ponderous freight cars into switches; trundling up and down, clanking, shrieking, their bells filling the air." Note that several airplanes have been dubbed into this postcard view as a way to further assert Chicago's modernity.

Not until the late twentieth century, with the coming of Amtrak, was rail passenger service in and out of Chicago finally coordinated at Union Station, located at West Adams and South Canal Streets. Like the Chicago and Northwestern Station, Union Station was a Beaux Arts creation, a classical monument to railroading. Although the architecture firm (Graham, Anderson, Probst and White) configured the station's main waiting room in marble, following a motif inspired by the Roman baths, they left the steel columns and girders in the concourse area bare (see **FIGURE 60**), giving the giant room a utilitarian grandeur. It was

through grand spaces such as this that most travelers entered Chicago. "In the terminal stations of the city," wrote Edward Hungerford, "you first begin to divine the real character of the city. You see it, a great crucible into which the people of all nations and all the corners of one of the greatest of the nations are being poured. Pressing her nose against the glass of a window that looks down into surpassingly busy streets, overshadowed by the ungainly bulk of an elevated railroad, is the bent figure of a hatless peasant woman from the south of Europe—seeing her America for the first time.... Next to her is a sleek, well-groomed man who may be from the East—from an Atlantic seaport city, but do not be too sure of that, for he may have his home over on Michigan avenue."

FIGURE 61 shows the Illinois Central Railroad's Twelfth Street Station, viewed from the north along Michigan Avenue. The Illinois Central was

FIGURE 61. The Twelfth Street Station from Michigan Avenue looking south, ca. 1910.

vital to the settling of much of Illinois beyond the metropolis, the company having received a huge federal land grant to build from Galena south to Cairo and from Chicago south to the IC line at Centralia. Abraham Lincoln once represented the railroad in court litigation, and his son, Robert Todd Lincoln, served for many years as the IC's chief executive officer. It was at the Twelfth Street Station that the vast majority of African Americans arrived from the South after the Civil War and well into the twentieth century. The impressive scene that greeted them, as pictured here at night about 1920, would have been more than a little exciting. Many, however, undoubtedly found it overwhelming, especially those who were just off impoverished sharecropper and tenant farms.

One of the Illinois Central's latter-day passenger trains is shown near the Twelfth Street Station in FIGURE 62. With the rise of both auto

and air travel, the nation's railroads modernized their passenger trains in order to remain competitive. New diesel-powered "streamlined" trains appeared: the "Rockets," the "Zephyrs," the "400s," the "Cities," the "Chiefs," the "Hiawathas." Of course, many early-twentieth-century nameplates remained: the Twentieth Century Limited, the Broadway Limited, the Empire State Builder.

Edgar Lee Masters recalled his first trip to Chicago: "I was wondering what Chicago would look like, how it would begin," he wrote. It had been difficult, he said, to tell exactly when the train left the prairie. It "bumped over the tracks of the outlying belt lines, where there was still farming country and widely separated houses. Then came the truck gardens of the city with houses closer together along half-made streets which stretched into vanishing distances of flat country. Then there were the new subdivisions springing

FIGURE 62. The Panama Limited, ca. 1950.

up all around, with newly built and half-finished apartment buildings and houses .... Factories, lumberyards, coalyards, grain elevators, tugs, sailing vessels, steamboats on the river and the canal swam into view as we rattled over switch tracks; and all around was the increasing density of the illimitable city, formed of miles of frame houses, lying cooked by the July sun and smothered in smoke and gas and smell, and in exhalation from the breweries, and in reeks from the stockyards."

Chicago was also an important radio city, second only to New York City in the production of original network programming. No program ever carried a stronger Chicago stamp than "Welcome Travelers," which aired over the American Broadcasting Company's Chicago affiliate, WLS (**FIGURE 63**). Travelers arriving in the city by train were invited to the Hotel Sherman, where, through informal conversation, their comings and goings were explored, invariably beginning with

the question "Why are you traveling today?" Thus was Chicago's importance as a railroad center publicized: images of travel in and out of the city carried to the nation as a media event. Chicago's clear-channel radio stations sent their signals out across the Midwest. WLS ("World's Largest Store") was originally owned by Sears, Roebuck and Company; WGN ("World's Greatest Newspaper") by the Tribune Company; and WCFL, calling itself "The Voice of Labor," by the Chicago Federation of Labor. One of the longest-running network series in radio history was "The Breakfast Club," originated by the National Broadcasting Company's WMAQ. Listeners were invited each morning to "march around the breakfast table."

In the early twentieth century, according to one guidebook, there were 800 miles of mainline railroad right-of-way in Chicago, and 1,400 miles of branch line. In total, they occupied 8 percent of the city's territory, or some 9,600 acres. By the

FIGURE 63. Promotional postcard for "Welcome Travelers," WLS radio, ca. 1950.

1920s, approximately 20 million freight cars were being shunted in and out of the city annually. It was said that one kind of train or another arrived or departed every minute of every hour of every day. The city's railroads were fully utilitarian: tracks (either depressed in cuts or, as was more usual, elevated along embankments) were lined with warehouses and factories (see **FIGURE 64**). In general, they did not offer the kind of scenery that postcard publishers cherished.

Seven major railroad corridors radiated out from the city's center, variously lined with warehouses and factories. In 1910, Chicago was home to some 9,700 manufacturing establishments, both large and small. They employed some 294,000 wage earners, more than the entire populations of rival gateway cities such as Kansas City and Omaha. Modest-sized industrial firms were rapidly on the rise. Many were established by immigrant entrepreneurs, often with foreign capital. For example, the Chicago firms established by Bernard Kuppenheimer and Joseph Schaffner were very well known in the garment industry. On factory floors, garment making was fragmented along ethnic and gender lines: most cutters, for example, were males of German or Irish descent, and tailors tended to be males from Sweden, Bohemia, or Russia, especially Russian Jews. Sewing machine operators, on the other hand, tended to be female, and from every background. Similar divisions of labor could be found in the printing industry: German Americans brought design and other technical skills from Europe, including North American patent rights to European printing processes; and native-born and immigrant Americans, especially women, handled the unskilled tasks in what amounted to assembly-line work.

Pictured in **FIGURE 65** is the Illinois Steel Company's South Chicago Works, part of the giant U.S. Steel conglomerate. As John and Ruth Ashenhurst

FIGURE 64. Railroad yard at Adams and Canal Streets, ca. 1910.

FIGURE 65. The South Chicago Works, Illinois Steel Company, ca. 1910.

noted, Chicago's steel mills were especially impressive when viewed at night: "The steel mills are not ordinarily open to visitors. But for a vivid picture of these workshops of Vulcan, you need only stand on any evening at such a vantage-point as the Ewing Avenue bridge over the Calumet River at Ninety-Second Street. A hundred black chimneys are silhouetted against the night sky, ruddy with the reflected light of vast furnaces." At South Chicago's giant Illinois Works, bright flames seen "spurting from its mighty blast furnaces" spread far into the night sky like "a southern Aurora Borealis."

Rarely celebrated in postcard art were the difficulties and dangers faced by industrial workers, be they employed in railroad shops, implement factories, or steel mills. Poor working conditions, long hours, and low pay sustained labor organizers in their endeavors decade after decade, but pictures of picket lines, for example, were simply not thought to be saleable as postcards. Nor did postcard publishers care to celebrate unemployment during periods of economic depression. Many of the nation's largest corporations had been founded in or were headquartered in Chicago, as were many of its largest labor unions, including the Amalgamated Clothing Workers of America and the United Steel Workers of America.

Nearly half of the nation's population lived within a night's train ride of Chicago. Chicago's hinterland, boosters asserted, was very much the "Great Central Market." Sears, Roebuck and Company was founded in 1886 when Richard W. Sears, a station agent in Minnesota, began selling watches through the mail to fellow railroad employees. Alvah Roebuck, a watch repairer, joined him. But it was Julius Rosenwald who, after buying out Roebuck, led the company to greatness. It was he who moved the firm into a giant west-side complex in Lawndale. The company became an important source of jobs for Jewish immigrants. Accordingly, Lawndale evolved mainly as a Jewish neighborhood. Rosenwald was a generous philanthropist, endowing both Jewish and African American charities. He founded Chicago's Museum of Science and Industry (see figure 87a). According to the caption on the back side of the postcard in FIGURE 66, the nine-story Merchandise Building, shown on the right, contained 2 million square feet of floor space from which some 9,000 employees sent out, on average, 200 carloads of merchandise daily. Second to Sears in the mail-order business was Montgomery Ward and Company, a firm initially established to serve the Patrons of Husbandry, better known as the Grange, a populist organization of farmers spread largely across the rural Midwest.

ETHNICITY AND RACE

Chicago had more than 780,000 foreign-born residents in 1910. Despite restrictions on immigration after World War I, that number climbed to over 859,00 in 1930. The 275,000 Jews living in Chicago in 1930 gave it the third-largest Jewish population in the world, behind Warsaw and New York City. The city's Jewish population was concentrated on the west side, with many families staying for generations. As social reformer Edith Abbott observed, "The clannishness of orthodox Jews from Russia which kept them so long in segregated, congested settlements was due in part to the fact that the refugee family first of all sought protection in semi-seclusion near the synagogue and the kosher markets—in a congregation of people 'from home.'" The Jewish market, centered at Halsted and Maxwell Streets, was especially important (FIGURE 67). After the fire of 1871, Jewish peddlers had flooded into the area to sell food, clothing, and other merchandise from backpacks, pushcarts, and wagons. The colorful market that evolved resembled an Eastern European bazaar, what many Americans may have envisioned Old World Jewish ghettos to have been like.

FIGURE 66. Sears, Roebuck and Company, ca. 1935.

FIGURE 67. Jewish market on Maxwell Street, ca. 1910.

FIGURE 68. Peddlers and merchants on Maxwell Street, ca. 1910.

Beyond, on the side streets, was what looked to most native-born Americans to be nothing more than a thriving slum. As defined by sociologist Harvey Zorbaugh, a slum is "a bleak area of segregation . . . , an area of extreme poverty, tenements, ramshackle buildings, of evictions and evaded rents; an area of working mothers and children, of high rates of birth, infant mortality, illegitimacy, and death; an area of pawnshops and second-hand stores, of gangs, of 'flops' where every bed is a vote." But what postcard publishers saw on Maxwell Street, and what they thought their customers wanted mostly to see, was the romance of an exotic marketplace.

Peddlers and merchants of varied backgrounds came to Maxwell Street to sell (FIGURE 68). But always the Jewish flavor remained. "The West Side has its so-called Ghetto," Robert Shackleton wrote, and there, especially on Sunday mornings, the ghetto dweller could be "picturesquely seen." "Then the street is packed and jammed with carts and boxes and stands, loaded with every variety of clothing, new and old; and one wonders where so many second-hand derby hats can possibly come from! . . . There is every variety of household utensil. There are dresses and jackets, and piles of cloth heaped directly upon the concrete pavement, and other piles on boards or paper. It is the most colorful street in Chicago, bright, brilliant, with every variety of glow." Observed Henry Justin Smith: "Along the sidewalks were masses of merchandise: live fowls in crates, rabbits and song-birds; sausages, bread and grains; slightly antique fur coats, overcoats, trousers, and more trousers." In the 1920s, Maxwell Street developed a reputation as a "thieves' market." Should one's hubcaps be stolen on Saturday night, one could likely buy them back on Maxwell Street the next morning.

Hull House, Chicago.

FIGURE 69. Hull House, ca. 1910.

Also residing on the city's near west side were Czechs, Irish, Italians, and Mexicans (largely Roman Catholic), as well as Greeks (largely Orthodox), most of them struggling to survive economically. "For depth of shadow in Chicago low life one must look to the foreign elements," advised Robert Woods. "Among them may be found a certain degree of isolation, and therefore of clannish crowding; also of contented squalor, jealous of inspection and interference." Hull House (**FIGURE 69**), the settlement house established by social reformer Jane Addams not far from Maxwell Street, was intended to break down newcomers' isolation and mistrust. Help was available there, especially the encouragement of self-help.

Hull House was the "flagship" for the nationwide settlement house movement. Ultimately some five hundred such places were opened in cities across the country. The Hull House staff established the city's first public playground and its first public bathhouse, campaigned to reform ward politics, and investigated city housing conditions. Staffers lobbied for improved sanitation, improved schools, and strict child labor and occupational safety laws. They helped establish the city's juvenile court system. Observed the Hungarian traveler Count Vay de Vaya and Luskod, "I was . . . deeply impressed by the arrangements of Hull House, which is administered by ladies of high culture, and is intended to form a centre for the promotion of intellectual pursuits among the working population of the neighbourhood, and for the material assistance of the deserving poor amongst them." Hull House symbolized the aggressive feminine side of a hard-nosed, commercially aggressive masculine city. The activities at Hull House epitomized the city's official motto: "I Will."

FIGURE 70. Family photo of two Polish women and a boy, 1917.

The flow of Poles into Chicago was primarily a peasant migration, initiated following the partition of Poland in the 1830s between Prussia, Russia, and Austria. A century later, the number of first-, second-, and third-generation Poles in Chicago was more than 500,000. Settling initially in north side neighborhoods that originally had been German-speaking, Chicago's Poles had dispersed by 1930, out along the long axis of Milwaukee Avenue northwest of downtown. A kind of American "Polonia" was located there, with a high density of churches, parochial schools, social clubs, mutual aid societies, and businesses all catering to Polish interests. Few postcard photographers ventured there. Existing postcard views, therefore, are mainly snapshot images taken by the people themselves and printed on postcard paper. Caught in a memorable moment in FIGURE 70 are two Polish women, likely with the son of one standing between them. Perhaps the two women are from

Minsk. The stage is set, the newspaper headline may be suggesting, for a new Polish state to be carved out of the wreckage of World War I.

Recently arrived migrants to Chicago rarely took pictures of their surroundings. First, few could afford the cameras and the film to do so. Also, most of their neighborhoods, being old and rundown, were not what they would have wanted to show each other, let alone relatives and friends back home. Working-class neighborhoods were not only flimsily built—houses cheaply rendered of balloon-frame construction—but, being near downtown, they were constantly threatened by the encroachment of commercial and industrial activities. Working-class neighborhoods seemed only to spiral downward: each wave of new people seemed less affluent, less educated, and with fewer prospects than those who had come before. Many observers would have agreed with novelist Mary Borden, who saw in Chicago's close-in neighbor-

FIGURE 71. Family photo, ca. 1920.

photos, including those sent as postcards, were mainly of family and friends (see **FIGURE 71**).

Pictured in **FIGURE 72** is the Meyer family in their front parlor on Chicago's north side. This photo, and the two that follow, came from the estate of Gilbert Meyer, the young man seated at the lower right. Here was an aspiring middle-class family of German descent and, judging by the room furnishings, a relatively affluent family, well-educated and with cultivated tastes. In 1900, some 470,000 Chicagoans either had been born in Germany or had a parent born there. Spread across the city's north side were the churches, the athletic clubs (the *turnvereins*), the music halls, the beer gardens, and the labor halls of a Chicago "Germania." Radical politics in Chicago was dominated by German socialists, although by the turn of the twentieth century, German radicalism was much in decline, supplanted by the bourgeois tendencies of families such as the Meyers. After the aborted 1848 revolution, many German-speakers had arrived in Chicago as artisans and craftsmen, their skills having been eclipsed by Germany's rapidly industrializing economy. Others came as small shopkeepers. Now, however, many of the succeeding generation, epitomized by Gilbert Meyer, were preparing to enter America's corporate managerial class.

"The visitor generally sees only the Loop, the Outer Drive, the Near North Side, the offices and hotels, and perhaps one or two institutions on the outskirts: factories, mail-order houses, university, hospitals," observed Graham Hutton. "He seldom sees the Chicagoans at home. Their homes are their pride, and rightly so," he emphasized. "Chicago has such oddities as houses with outside wooden steps up to the second-story front doors. . . . The homes are detached, instead of being built closely shoulder to shoulder," wrote Robert Shackleton. In the snapshot in **FIGURE 73**, members of the Meyer family are posing behind their home,

hoods "thousands upon thousands of new, shabby, square wooden boxes, no more solid than packing cases, perched on the hard ground. They look as if the icy wind would blow them away, and round them, between them, are vacant lots, ragged patches of prairie littered with scrap-iron, stones, and garbage." What begged to be remembered, and to be photographed, were the people, and especially the good times they enjoyed. Despite the challenges of being in a strange new land, most immigrants found life in America promising. Snapshot

FIGURE 72. Meyer family photo, ca. 1905.

FIGURE 73. Meyer family photo, ca. 1905.

FIGURE 74. Meyer family backyard, ca. 1905.

ible. The next-door neighbor on the left appears to have been affluent enough to keep a horse and a carriage, the corner of a stable being visible. Poking up in the distance are the roofs and turrets of business buildings on a commercial street, perhaps North Avenue. "North Avenue is still a northern European thoroughfare," wrote sociologist Harvey Zorbaugh. "Its many German cafes—Wein Stube (with a bunch of huge gilded grapes over the door), Pilsner, Wur'n Sepp Family Resort, Komiker Sepp—give it a distinctive color. . . . The windows of the many delicatessen shops plainly proclaim Swiss, German, or Hungarian; and they have little tables about which men eat lunches of rye bread, sauerkraut, sausage, pickles, perhaps with alpenkrauter, and talk in German." Swedes, Norwegians, and Danes were also numerous on Chicago's north side. According to Julian Ralph, the Scandinavians were known to "quickly and easily follow and adopt every Americanism. In return, they ask only to be permitted to attend a host of Lutheran churches in flocks, to work hard, live temperately, save thriftily, and to pronounce every *j* as if it were a *y*."

Not every immigrant family thrived. Illness (and even death), unemployment (or underemployment), stressed marriages, and deserting spouses were all too common. So too were children who were difficult to control, caught as they were between old and new lifeways. Juvenile delinquency was universal across the city's working-class neighborhoods. Chicago was thus one of the first American cities to develop a separate justice system for juvenile offenders. The city also established the Chicago Parental School, where the more incorrigible, including the truant, could be removed from their families and, under a regime of steady discipline, set upon a path to presumed righteousness (**FIGURE 75**). The Chicago Parental School was run as a military academy, with the senior students, as cadet officers, taking responsi-

a space that offered some privacy but that was also fully utilitarian, although German neatness is evident in the yard's high level of maintenance.

In **FIGURE 74**, a photo taken out of a side window of the Meyer home, perhaps by Gilbert Meyer himself, we see across the back lots of their north side neighborhood. It was probably the fresh snowfall that interested the photographer. Utility sheds and a few dormant fruit trees are vis-

FIGURE 75. Playground, Chicago Parental School, 1918.

bility for disciplining the younger boys. With the United States a combatant in the "Great European War," the military emphasis provided a special opportunity to teach patriotism, and thus instill in students distinctly American values and ideals. Their parents were encouraged to attend night school, often under threat of losing their jobs, to learn English and be "good Americans." Once the United States entered the war, many German Americans found it politic to speak only English and to anglicize their names.

The photographs from the Chicago Parental School were taken by two teachers there, Grant and Emma Thornton. For years they photographed their students, accompanying each photo with a brief biographical sketch. FIGURE 76, for example, shows "James Brown, 11227 Stephenson Ave. First time here. Father Cherokee Indian. Mother colored. Born Oct. 3, 1900." Although African Ameri-

cans made up less than 3 percent of Chicago's population in 1900, the black community provided more than 50 percent of the city's low-paid servants. It was usually only as strikebreakers that black males obtained factory work, in which case they incurred the hostility of white workers. Once strikes were settled, of course, whites were usually rehired and strikebreakers let go, leaving blacks not only unemployed, but living with heightened racial prejudice.

In 1920, some 40,000 African Americans, approximately 70 percent of all blacks in the city, lived on Chicago's south side, in an area one to two blocks wide and some thirty blocks long, sandwiched between the mainlines of the Illinois Central and the Rock Island Railroads. There, according to Henry Justin Smith, "the pedestrians are of all shades of darkness, and all degrees of neatness or shabbiness. On the corners are apt

Building, completed in 1905, which housed the city's main post office, the district federal court, and the offices of various federal agencies (FIGURE 77). Designed by Henry Ives Cobb, the Beaux Arts building took the outline of a Greek cross upon which was placed a majestic dome, larger than the one on the U.S. Capitol in Washington, D.C. It was in this building that the Standard Oil Trust was broken up in 1911. One of its descendant companies, Standard Oil of Indiana, operated the nation's largest oil refinery just across the Indiana border at Whiting, a focus of the government's suit. In 1931, Al Capone was convicted and sentenced in the Federal Building. Organized crime was closely associated with the city, especially during Prohibition. Events such as the St. Valentine's Day Massacre, in which seven gangsters were killed in a hail of machine gun bullets in a north side garage, made headlines worldwide. The courthouse was an impressive structure. "Though closely hedged in on three sides by great skyscrapers, making it difficult to get the full effect, the Federal Building is without doubt one of the most pleasing and imposing public buildings in this country," said *A Guide to the City of Chicago* in 1909. "Entering from either Clark, Dearborn or Adams St. the visitor passes through a spacious corridor into a great rotunda under the main dome. (Distance from floor to top of dome 139 feet.)"

Following the 1871 fire, a large government building was erected to house both city and county offices. Rendered in French Second Empire style, it was designed to surpass Philadelphia City Hall, where city and county governments were actually integrated. Pictured in FIGURE 78 is the entry hall of the replacement building of 1905, a Beaux Arts structure designed by Holabird and Roche. The dignitaries in formal attire add to a sense of the building's splendor. Community pride was celebrated in civic architecture everywhere across the nation, but few cities could afford the kind of lav-

to be seen pausing, gazing about with eyes half opened to the opportunities of their adopted city, new-comers from the South, families straight from little cabins in Mississippi or Alabama. Some still carry the bundles that contain all they own." Commercial postcards rarely depicted African Americas, but when they did, it was usually done "humorously" by parodying one or another racial stereotype.

GOVERNMENT

The large government buildings that graced downtown more than held their own amid the city's skyscrapers. None surpassed the Federal

FIGURE 77. The United States Courthouse, Chicago, 1910.

FIGURE 78. Chicago City Hall and the Cook County Courthouse, 1910.

FIGURE 79. The Coliseum, South Wabash Avenue, ca. 1910.

ish structure that Chicago built. No postcard publisher could avoid picturing such an obvious civic gesture. Cook County was named for congressman Daniel P. Cook, who, as one of Illinois's earliest politicians of note, helped arrange statehood.

The structure at right in FIGURE 79 was the second amphitheater to carry the name "Coliseum," its castellated entry pavilion an enthusiastic gesture to romantic monumentality. Several Republican national conventions were held there in the early twentieth century: in 1904 (at which Theodore Roosevelt was nominated for president), 1908 (William Howard Taft), 1912 (Taft again), 1916 (Charles Evans Hughes), and 1920 (Warren G. Harding). In 1912, Theodore Roosevelt broke with the Republicans to form the Progressive Party. His "Bull Moose" campaign, which split the Republican vote and put Woodrow Wilson in the White House, was launched at Chicago's Auditorium Building. Democrats also met in Chicago. Edgar

Lee Masters recalled the 1896 Democratic Convention, held at the Coliseum's predecessor building. "It was a spectacle never to be forgotten," he wrote. "It was the beginning of a changed America. Bryan's voice, so golden and winning, came clearly to my ears as he said, 'You shall not press down upon the brow of labor this crown of thorns, you shall not crucify mankind upon a cross of gold.'" Bryan, whose political career was anchored in Nebraska, was born and raised in Salem, Illinois.

FIGURE 80 shows the Cook County Hospital as it looked in 1905. "This group of buildings," read a Chicago guidebook, "is in itself one of the most prophetic things about Chicago. That cities a hundred years old have not made the philanthropical efforts that are here recorded within twenty years demonstrates the growing power of the West." The hospital's 1874 administration building is pictured here, along with the various appendages added over the years, including the

FIGURE 80. Cook County Hospital, ca. 1905.

children's wing and the detention hospital ("here the insane are kept awaiting the sessions of the court"). "The hospital cares for about 1,100 patients daily," another guidebook reported twelve years later. "No money is taken from patients for treatment of any sort, the hospital being maintained entirely by taxation." It added: "The County Morgue is just to the rear of the hospital and may be viewed freely." The nation's first blood bank was established at this hospital, and the nation's first medical internship program was begun there. The clientele consisted primarily of the city's poor, especially European immigrants. After World War I, the African American community developed a substantial dependence on the facility, given the policies of racial exclusion practiced at most of the city's other hospitals.

Although the University of Chicago was privately endowed, it performed many important public services, operating one of the city's largest hospitals, for example. Marshall Field donated much of the land, and John D. Rockefeller much of the money, for the new University of Chicago, built north of the Midway Plaisance, a mile-long strip of land where an entertainment zone had been located during the World's Columbian Exposition, complete with the "Streets of Cairo" and the original Ferris Wheel. The campus, as depicted in FIGURE 81, contained some thirty buildings spread over ninety-five acres, most of them arrayed around one of six quadrangles. Edna Ferber, in her novel *So Big*, described the university's campus, calling it Midwest University: "You heard such wonderful things about [it]. . . . those Gothic buildings gave an effect, somehow, of age and permanence (the smoke and cinders from the Illinois Central suburban trains were largely responsible for that, as well as the soft coal from a thousand neighboring chimneys). And there actually was ivy. Undeniable ivy, and mullioned

FIGURE 81. The University of Chicago, ca. 1935.

windows." Robert Shackleton found things much like his native England: "With corbels and crockets and pinnacles, with floors of oak and stairways of oak, with feudal-looking entrances and passages, with sun-dials and gargoyles and stone turrets and wrought-iron gates, with friezes of stone, with oriel windows and windows casemented, with buttresses . . . , with ancient-seeming stone bridges between buildings, there is wealth of fascinating detail." Symbolized was a Chicago cultured, perhaps, like an Oxford or a Cambridge.

LEISURE TIME

Pictured in **FIGURE 82** is a 1904 football game under way in the University of Chicago stadium. A handwritten message reads: "Directly in front of where we sat. Eckessall ready for the punt. 63–0 Wow!" The university's athletic teams played in the Western Athletic Conference (the Big Ten) until 1929, when Robert Maynard Hutchins became university president. His "new plan" for the

university eliminated intercollegiate sports and emphasized scholarship. The football stadium, however, gained prominence during World War II as the site of the world's first self-sustaining nuclear chain reaction, an event that may be said to have initiated the "nuclear age." The experiment, which took place at 3:25 P.M. on December 2, 1942, in a converted squash court under the stands, was conducted by physicist Enrico Fermi as part of the Manhattan Project, which produced the first atomic bomb.

Commercial piers and bathhouses gave ordinary Chicagoans access to Lake Michigan. In **FIGURE 83**, a Sunday crowd is enjoying the Windsor Bathing Beach on the city's south side, most of them wading or just walking around rather than swimming, there to see and be seen. Appearing in public, especially on a Sunday, dictated a degree of formal dress. Attire helped to establish and maintain class distinctions: to separate, for example, the native from the foreigner. Postcard publishers

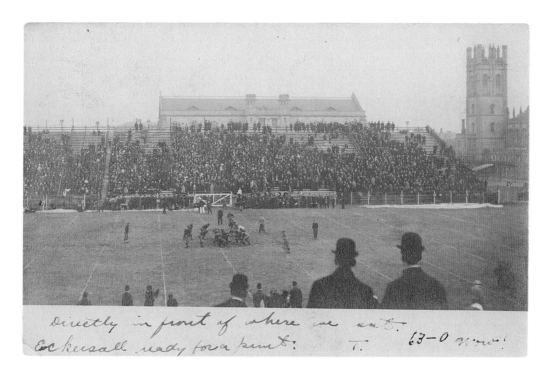

directly in front of where we sat. Eckersall ready for a punt. T. 63—0 wow!

FIGURE 82. The University of Chicago football stadium, 1904.

Windsor Bathing Beach, Lake Michigan.
View from 75th Street, Chicago

FIGURE 83. The Windsor Bathing Beach, 1910.

Outer Harbor and Recreation Pier, Chicago.

"Copyrighted 1915, by Max Rigot, Chicago"

FIGURE 84. Recreation Pier and Outer Harbor, 1916.

were usually careful to depict well-dressed people in city streets. Like the picturing of fashionable architecture, the picturing of polite dress spoke, by analogy, of a quality of place. But in this scene some informality is clearly noticeable as well. Observed Edward Hungerford: "On pleasant summer days, [Chicagoans] go bathing in the lake by the thousands, and if they live within half a dozen blocks of the shore they will go and come in their bathing suits, with perhaps a light coat or bathrobe thrown over them. A man from New York might be shocked . . . ; but that is Chicago."

Chicago's lakefront was the scene of much social tension. The beaches were segregated during those years. On July 27, 1919, a race riot broke out in the city. It was precipitated by whites who threw rocks at some black bathers, killing one. In the ensuing melee, which spread across the city, twenty-three blacks and fifteen whites died,

hundreds of both races were injured, and property damage was immense due to arson and looting. Civil disorder, especially of the violent kind, was hardly what postcard publishers wanted to portray. Cities such as Chicago needed to be depicted as progressive and prosperous, if not liberal-minded. **FIGURE 84** shows what came to be known as Navy Pier. Although the 1909 *Plan of Chicago* called for several such structures to be built out into the lake, this was the only one that was completed. Opened in 1916, it was intended to service lake shipping, but also to be a public entertainment venue. The 3,000-foot-long pier was organized on three levels: the lowest for handling freight, the middle for lake boat passengers, and the upper for pedestrian promenading. A promotional pamphlet produced by the Illinois Central Railroad offered this description: "At the lakeward end is a gigantic auditorium and dance pavilion,

FIGURE 85. Lincoln Park, ca. 1905.

with facilities for picnics, children's playgrounds, refectories, and art rooms; two stately towers, with observation galleries, rise from the Pier and afford comprehensive views of Chicago's water traffic. Band concerts are given during the summer, and dancing is enjoyed." The personal message written on the back of this postcard reads: "Wish you might spend the day in Chicago and go out on this pier. . . . Out at the end [we] had plenty of cold sodas and ice cream. Have been having one grand time since we came here. Cousin Lydia."

The city's largest cemetery, located north of downtown on the lakefront, was recognized by public health officials as a source of water contamination, leading to cholera and other epidemics. In the 1860s, a crusade was launched to move the graves and convert the area to a park, which ultimately became Lincoln Park (**FIGURE 85**). Three separate park commissions were established by the State of Illinois in 1869, to oversee park development for the northern, southern, and westerns portions of the city, respectively. Frederick Law Olmsted and Calvert Vaux, the architects of New York City's Central Park, designed Jackson and Washington Parks on the south side. Chicago architect William Le Baron Jenny designed Humboldt, Garfield, and Douglas Parks on the west side, all of which landscape gardener Jens Jensen later modified in a more naturalistic "prairie style." Landscape architect Swain Nelson designed Lincoln Park.

With their curved carriage drives, lagoons, and carefully contrived vistas, Lincoln and the other parks celebrated the nineteenth-century aesthetic of the picturesque. They were meant to be passively driven or walked through and looked at. After 1900, however, active recreation, especially organized sport, was increasingly accommodated:

FIGURE 86. Advertising postcard for the White City Amusement Park, ca. 1900.

picnic grounds, baseball fields, and other amenities, such as field houses, were added. Lincoln Park, of course, was named for the martyred president, whom most Chicagoans had come to consider one of their own—something that Robert Shackleton found curious: "It was a Chicago convention that set him on his way to the Presidency. He was of Illinois, and all Illinois—that is, so much of it as the city cares for—is taken, quite casually, as being of Chicago. The city so ignores the State as a separate entity that, whereas you will hear the word 'Chicago' on the lips of Chicagoans a thousand times a day, you will hear the word 'Illinois' scarcely once in a year."

The 1893 World's Columbian Exposition helped redefine how Americans spent their leisure time. It was not the fair's culturally refined aspect that dominated, with its Beaux Arts architecture (see figure 8). Rather, it was the amusement section, the Midway Plaisance, with its Ferris Wheel, fun houses, and other attractions brightly lit at night. Elements of the Midway Plaisance lived on at the White City Amusement Park after the fair closed (FIGURE 86). As one Chicago guidebook noted: "White City is a noted amusement park with a picturesque group of white buildings crowned by spires, towers, cupolas, and minarets. Its attractions include coasters, scenic railways, chute-the-chutes, fun houses, Ferris wheel, skating rinks, shooting galleries, dance pavilion, bandstand, restaurant, theatre, and many other features." In Chicago, as across America, new forms of popular culture were evolving, including cinema, radio, and recorded music, cultural forms derived not so much from an elite pursuit of social status as from a popular pursuit of excitement: bright night lights, the exhilaration of speed, and the embrace of novelty for novelty's sake.

FIGURE 87A. The Museum of Science and Industry, ca. 1940.

The Palace of Fine Arts in Jackson Park was also built for the World's Columbian Exposition. In 1926, the structure was stripped of its plaster and given a veneer of stone, and its walls and floors were reinforced with steel beams. A lagoon was created, reminiscent of the fair's Court of Honor. According to the caption, the postcard in FIGURE 87A shows "the colossal structure in its landscaped setting." "Now rebuilt, it contains a full-size operating bituminous coal mine, in addition to other machine age masterpieces in operation." The idea was not only to celebrate the advance of modern technology but to showcase those specific advances that had been made in Chicago, as well as downstate. The Museum of Science and Industry opened in 1933, the year of Chicago's second World's Fair ("A Century of Progress International Exposition"), which celebrated the city's centennial. Besides the working coal mine, other favorite exhibits included the first Zephyr streamlined train (originally put in operation by the Chicago,

Burlington and Quincy Railroad about the time of the museum's opening) and the German submarine U-505, which had been captured in World War II. The caption on the postcard in FIGURE 87B reads: "Among the physics displays are many devices which make it easier to learn about magnetism and electricity." But the personal message on the back strikes a different note. The card was addressed to Bozo Circus, c/o WGN-TV Channel Nine, Chicago, Illinois. La Tanja Jence Burrell (319 E. Flagg St., Aurora, Illinois, 60505), two and a half years old, was applying to make her first television appearance as an audience member.

A Century of Progress, held at the height of the Great Depression, was an anticipation of better times to come. The fair was built on newly filled land south of the Shedd Aquarium and east of Soldier Field. Its board of directors was headed by Rufus G. Dawes, president of the Pure Oil Company. Employment in Chicago's factories at the time was down by half. Real estate foreclosures were

FIGURE 87B. The Museum of Science and Industry, ca. 1965.

soaring, and land values were tumbling. Chicago and the nation needed encouragement, if only of the symbolic kind. Theater designer Joseph Urban, along with architects Louis Skidmore and Nathaniel Owings, adopted a futuristic vision for the exposition. Exhibition buildings, massed geometrics with plain surfaces and rounded corners, were rendered in Streamline Moderne style, the same styling that had already come to characterize airplanes, automobiles, passenger trains, and even refrigerators. Buildings were painted in pastel hues and were brightly lit at night. Indeed, the fair was deliberately designed for nighttime viewing.

The exposition's main attraction was the Sky Ride, with its "rocket cars" that ran on cables suspended between two towers on either side of a large lagoon (**FIGURE 88**). "These huge steel skeleton towers rise 618 feet above the ground level," wrote two visitors to the fair. "Fast elevators take passengers to observatories at the top, from which on clear days four States may be seen—Illinois, Indiana, Michigan, and Wisconsin." They dutifully relayed the exposition's main message: that problems, no matter how grave, could be solved through engineering. Had not tremendous strides been made since Chicago's previous fair forty years earlier? "Within this short period," they wrote, "man has learned to fly, to talk across the ocean without wires, to produce artificial climate in homes and offices, to make ice with a gas flame. Moreover, his attitude has changed. In 1933 men of science know that nothing is impossible—that man has not reached a pinnacle but has merely stepped across another threshold."

Chicagoans were increasingly turning to organized sport, especially to baseball, both as participants and, more particularly, as spectators. Chicago's first professional baseball team, the

FIGURE 88. Promotional postcard for the Century of Progress International Exposition, 1933.

White Stockings, was launched in 1870. Renamed the Cubs, the club became the only National League franchise to play every season in the city of its founding. Wrigley Field was built in 1918. Bought along with the team by William Wrigley two years later, it has remained the centerpiece of one of Chicago's distinctive neighborhoods, Wrigleyville. In the view of the stadium in FIGURE 89, the surroundings have all but been eliminated through retouching, a common technique used by postcard publishers to place the emphasis on architecture. With its population doubling each decade through the 1890 census, and with more than a half-million new residents being added each decade thereafter through the Great Depression, Chicago could, and did, support other professional baseball teams, most importantly the White Sox of the American League, but also the American Giants of the National Negro League.

LIVING IN THE CITY

Chicago's residential neighborhoods ranged from extreme wealth to extreme poverty, with most falling somewhere in between. Prairie Avenue, on the south side, was the city's most exclusive residential address through the 1890s. Here lived Marshall Field and George Pullman, among other luminaries. The postcard in FIGURE 90 shows the 1887 home of farm implement manufacturer John Glessner at right, designed by Boston architect H. H. Richardson in his signature Romanesque Revival style. After 1900, the area's proximity to the Illinois Central Railroad on the east and to the city's notorious vice district, the Levee, on the west encouraged Chicago's elite families to settle elsewhere, especially north of downtown along Lake Michigan. By 1930, Prairie Avenue was but a shell of its former self. In the words of Henry Justin Smith, "Old Prairie Avenue is a street of

Wrigley Field, Home of the Chicago Cubs

162

FIGURE 89. Wrigley Field, ca. 1940.

FIGURE 90. Prairie Avenue, ca. 1900.

FIGURE 91. Lake Shore Drive, ca. 1900.

ghosts and ghost-houses. A wind of desolation blows through it. Such of the old mansions as have not been taken over for offices or rooming-houses stand stoutly, brazening out old age and desertion, some with boarded windows, a few with shattered panes. Marshall Field's granary-like edifice, of red brick with mansard roof, under whose porte-cochere broughams used to arrive with a creak of harness, remains, with a haughty stare for neighbors; and the garden at one side is a barren yard." Marshall Field's house had been the first in Chicago to be lit by electricity.

North Lake Shore Drive was next to become Chicago's most exclusive residential address. Pictured on the left in FIGURE 91 is Potter and Bertha Palmer's mansion, a Henry Ives Cobb–designed castle of sandstone and granite that was completed in 1888. Lake Shore Drive was, observed Henry Justin Smith, "the right place to live" for the children and grandchildren of the city's founders. He wrote: "They are grouped closely, these folk who count as social thoroughbreds, on a tier of streets whose golden attributes are laid on only a few blocks from east to west; a tier whose length, from south to north, is a doubtful mile." "The real leaders of Chicago society," Robert Shackleton reported, "are people, mostly of great wealth, who are cultured, alert and intelligent, unpretentious and unassuming; even though the men may have won world-wide fame in connection with beef or banks, soap or sleeping-cars." "There is," he added, "much of a breezy openness of life; and I have seen women, of undoubted high standing, freely and breezily powder their faces in public."

Gentry neighborhoods, although hardly as pretentious, also evolved southward, even along Michigan Avenue (FIGURE 92)—although well below the car dealerships arrayed close to downtown that marked Chicago's first "automobile row." The south side's broad avenues and landscaped boulevards attracted a prospering upper middle class, composed of small business owners, professional

FIGURE 92. Michigan Avenue at Thirty-Fifth Street, ca. 1907.

people, and the managerial class of the city's large corporations, especially those whose businesses were located south of downtown. The boulevards were favored as recreational carriageways and, after 1900, as streets to motor on. "What other city has begun so nobly or has planned so liberally for metropolitan solidity, elegance, and recreation?" asked the author of a history of Chicago. "Chicago is a city of detached houses, in the humbler quarters as well as in the magnificent avenues, and the effect is home-like and beautiful at the same time. There is great variety, stone, brick, and wood intermingled, plain and ornamental; but drive where you will in the favorite residence parts of the vast city, you will be continually surprised with the sight of noble and artistic houses and homes displaying taste as well as luxury." Initially, the automobile was a plaything for Chicago's wealthy. For them, motoring was primarily a recreational activity at first, often undertaken as a sporting event. The nation's first automobile race was organized by a city newspaper as a publicity stunt.

Millard Avenue in Lawndale was typical of the more affluent working-class neighborhoods that developed in Chicago around 1900 (**FIGURE 93**). It was a street of two-story "flats," buildings that sported separate apartments on each floor. "Flat fever" had produced small, tenement-like apartment buildings throughout the city, originally scattered along the main streets with streetcar lines, and then built shoulder to shoulder up and down the side streets. Buildings were put up on speculation by small contractors, each tending to replicate a given building plan over and over again, resulting in a great deal of uniformity. Upton Sinclair placed the two main characters of *The Jungle* in such an apartment. "They were on a street which seemed to run on forever, mile after mile—thirty-four of them, if they had known it—and each side of it one uninterrupted row of wretched little two-story frame buildings. Down every side street they could see, it was the same,—never a hill and never a hollow, but always the same endless vista of ugly and dirty little wooden

FIGURE 93. Millard Avenue, Lawndale, ca. 1910.

buildings." Lawndale, however, was a little more upscale: its flats were of brick.

Factory work meant unskilled, low-paying jobs. The increasingly radicalized labor movement that emerged in response seemed to threaten the very foundations of Chicago's economic successes. Decent housing and, more importantly, home ownership appeared key to improved labor-management relations. If workers owned their own homes, or so the argument went, they would consider that they held a stake in industrial society irrespective of the social inequalities inherent to it. Indeed, low-priced lumber, continued reliance on balloon-frame construction, cheap labor, and the evolution of the building and loan industry did foster high levels of home ownership, not only in Chicago, but nationwide. Most Chicagoans, nonetheless, continued to rent, especially unmarried

workers, who tended to live in rooming houses or to board with others. Renting out a spare bedroom, especially to a relative, was one way a struggling family could improve their finances.

Pictured in **FIGURE 94** is an interior decor that a working-class family in Chicago might have aspired to: the fireplace a symbol of warm family tradition, and the piano evidence of uplifted culture. The printed message on the back of the card reads: "Dear Madam: Springtime is Wall Paper Time! When would you like to see the new styles for 1908, fresh from Chicago? A large line to select from. Orders by mail or telephone promptly attended to. No trouble to show goods." One's residence, and its furnishings and decor, symbolized success among working-class families. And, indeed, those who had worked their way up into the lower echelons of corporate management did

A SUGGESTION TO BEAUTIFY YOUR HOME
Selection from Remien & Kuhnert Co.'s New Sample Books, Chicago. Wouldn't Something Like This Lend Charm To Your Room-

FIGURE 94. Advertising postcard for the Remien and Kuhnert Company, 1900.

live rather well. The philosopher Walter Pitkin wrote: "It is the rule rather than the exception that a cheap wooden house will contain, among other things, a $500 piano or automatic player piano, a $150 radio, a $50 talking machine, and a $50 icebox (the latter now rapidly being displaced by $200 electric refrigerators). There is usually a good bathroom, usually with a shower, and almost always there is central heating, with hot and cold water upstairs and down. All these are bought on installments which run from one to five years."

Apartment living became an important alternative both in Chicago and in its suburbs. Many buildings were operated as "co-ops," especially in lakefront neighborhoods north of downtown but also south along the lake, especially in Hyde Park near the University of Chicago. Rather than own an individual unit, as with a condominium, the members of a cooperative shared in the owner-

ship of an entire building. Unfortunately, during the Great Depression, more than three-quarters of the city's cooperatives went into receivership. The Seville, however, was a commercial apartment hotel, its tenants strictly renters. It offered services beyond those expected in mere apartment houses. The caption on the postcard in FIGURE 95 reads: "Fireproof and Soundproof. 1, 2, 3 room furnished kitchenette apartments, living room 13 x 18 feet. Separate dining room and kitchen; large dressing room. Bath with shower. Ice, gas, electricity, linen and maid service. Telephone in every room: 24 hour service. Bus stops at door." The most popular apartment buildings had three- or four-story U-shaped plans. They had a "deeply recessed center and projecting wings, and with the space between the wings charmingly cared for with grass and walks and shrubbery," wrote Robert Shackleton. "People nowadays want a stylish home," the

FIGURE 95. The Seville Apartment Hotel, ca. 1925.

FIGURE 96. The Edgewater Beach Hotel, ca. 1930.

FIGURE 97. The Chicago Temple, ca. 1935.

was the work of a single developer, John Lewis Cochran. He subdivided the area by extending the established Chicago street grid northward. On large lots along the lakefront, he encouraged the construction of large houses and, later on, apartment buildings. Many second- and third-generation German, Irish, and Scandinavian families came to Edgewater, part of the northward drift of those seeking escape from older, declining neighborhoods. In 1916 Cochran built the Edgewater Beach Hotel, to which a tall apartment tower was added in 1929. The caption on the postcard in FIGURE 96 states: "World renowned for its superb location on Lake Michigan . . . with more than a thousand feet of the finest beach and beach promenade, out-of-door dancing on a marble floor. Every up to date convenience for summer or permanent guests. Gardens, children's playgrounds, tennis and golf putting course. Its Marine Dining Room is unsurpassed. A 200-car garage in the hotel. Private motor coach service to shopping center over Outer Drive in fifteen minutes."

RELIGION

Chicago was a city of churches. Indeed, church spires dominated the skyline through to the last decade of the nineteenth century. Downtown, of course, high-rise buildings tended to obscure the churches from view when they did not replace them altogether. One church building that held its own was the Chicago Temple, depicted in the nighttime view in FIGURE 97 as seemingly reaching for the cosmos. Home to the city's First Methodist Church, the skyscraper building, designed by Holabird and Roche in a French Gothic style, contained a large church auditorium (with the world's largest organ), a gymnasium, Sunday school rooms and church offices on the lower floors, and rental office space on the floors above. At the top was the Chapel in the Sky. At 556 feet, the Chicago Temple was the fifth-tallest building

novelist Robert Herrick observed, "with elevator boys in uniform. . . . That court you've got there between the wings, and the little fountain, and the grand entrance—all just right."

Edgewater was located some seven miles north of the Loop. Like many of Chicago's suburbs, it was unable to supply its own water and other utilities at low cost, so its residents eventually agreed to be annexed by the City of Chicago. Edgewater

FIGURE 98. The Moody Bible Institute, ca. 1930.

in the world when it was completed in 1923. According to a city guidebook, "In the building there are 25 miles of electric conduit, 60 miles of single wire, 8 miles of plumbing pipes, 925 radiators, 2,000,000 bricks, 125,000 pieces of Bedford [Indiana] stone, 21 acres of plastering." The caption on the back of this postcard champions the structure as "the world's tallest church."

Churches and synagogues played an important role in the city's social life. Many newly arrived immigrant families sought to join a congregation where their native language was spoken, and where familiar Old World customs were retained. The Roman Catholics and the Lutherans, in particular, established parochial schools to further knit together ethnically based religious communities. There were also numerous convents and church-run orphanages and asylums in the city. Many of the hospitals were also affiliated with churches. Established in and around Chicago were

some of the nation's largest and most influential seminaries, including the McCormick Theological Seminary, which served the Presbyterians.

Reminiscent, perhaps, of the Byzantine Hagia Sophia in Istanbul, the Moody Bible Institute's unusual red brick building was completed in 1925 (FIGURE 98). Evangelical Protestantism blossomed in Chicago. Founded in 1889 by Dwight Moody and Emma Dryer, the institute became one of the nation's largest missionary training centers, its initial purpose being to "fill the gaps" between ordinary people and the established clergy out in Chicago's neighborhoods. It especially supported proselytizing among Chicago's Jews and Roman Catholics. The ultimate goal of the Moody Institute was to counter liberal Protestant theology through the fostering of conservative, Bible-oriented Christian fundamentalism. Moody had earlier helped found the Young Men's Christian Association (the YMCA). Two other prominent

FIGURE 99. St. Mary of the Lake Seminary, Mundelein, ca. 1930.

twentieth-century evangelists were also closely associated with Chicago: Billy Sunday played baseball in the city in earlier years, and Billy Graham began his worldwide "crusades" while he was living in suburban Wheaton.

Roman Catholics, organized both in territorial and in "national" (or ethnically based) parishes, constituted the city's largest religious group. The Chicago Archdiocese became especially noteworthy for both its size and its activism, with a series of prelates who proved to be highly competent institution builders through their promotion of progressive social agendas. Prime among them was George William Cardinal Mundelein, the archbishop of Chicago from 1916 to 1939. It was he who organized the 1926 Eucharistic Congress, extraordinary at the time with its mass meeting of some 125,000 people staged in Soldier Field. He also established St. Mary of the Lake Seminary (today's Mundelein Seminary), pictured in FIGURE 99, and promoted Chicago's two Roman Catholic universities, DePaul and Loyola.

CHICAGO'S SUBURBS

Methodists in Chicago established the North Western University in the Loop in the 1850s, opening a branch several years later twelve miles to the north, fronting on Lake Michigan. There the suburb of Evanston evolved. Its charter, influenced by the church, prohibited the sale of alcoholic beverages. As a quiet retreat from Chicago, Evanston became one of the city's most affluent suburbs. Championed one guidebook: "The town because of its size, beauty and many advantages deserves more than passing notice. It is purely a residential and college town, known the country over for its clean streets, beautiful homes, fine shade trees and splendidly kept lawns." Resident

FIGURE 100. Fountain Square, Evanston, ca. 1925.

writer Marian White found Evanston "a beautiful city, ideal in its preservation of the forest trees.... There are many beautiful homes here, many dear, old-fashioned structures, as well as those of more modern design and imposing appearance; but all in an environment of emerald lawn, graceful shrub, clinging vine and stately trees." Commuters could ride downtown on railroad, electric interurban, or mass transit trains. Evanston's downtown, oriented to commuting, centered around Fountain Square (FIGURE 100).

"Northwestern University is making a distinct contribution in reducing wickedness and increasing right doing," wrote the university's president, Walter Dill Scott, in 1929. The institution's suburban location, with its large, park-like campus (FIGURE 101A), quickly assumed primacy over its older, much smaller downtown location, although a medical campus did evolve in "Streeterville," just east of Michigan Avenue along the lake on the city's near north side. Evanston was promoted as the ideal place for educating youth. It was away from the corrupting influences of the central city and yet not so far away that students and faculty could not partake of Chicago's cultural resources. It was well situated to serve the sons and daughters of Chicago's elite families, especially those who had relocated to the prestigious "North Shore."

Various Protestant denominations, along with organizations such as the Woman's Christian Temperance Union (the WCTU), led the fight against a host of perceived social evils, especially the consumption of alcohol. Organized in 1874, the WCTU selected the charismatic Frances E. Willard as its president five year later. FIGURE 101B shows Willard's Evanston home, which became a symbol of American middle-class propriety. The temperance movement, which gave rise to other causes, especially civil rights and women's suffrage, led eventually to national Prohibition. The Prohibition movement was clearly strengthened by the

FIGURE 101A. Northwestern University, ca. 1900.

FIGURE 101B. Frances Willard's home, Rest Cottage, Evanston, ca. 1905.

FIGURE 102. Greenwood Avenue, Wilmette, ca. 1910.

anti-immigrant hysteria that swept the country during and after World War I, when a peacetime nation presumed to want "normalcy." In 1920, well over 50 percent of Illinois's population was of German, Irish, Scandinavian, or eastern or southern European descent. The cultural differences between "native-born" and "foreign-born" Illinoisans loomed large, as the controversy over drinking suggested. Illinois's unsuccessful fight against the "anti-saloon" crowd was led by the leader of the Czech community, Anton Cermak, who later served as one of Chicago's most well-respected mayors.

"If the beauty, majesty and grandeur of this city strike with wonder all who gaze upon it for the first time," wrote the author of a Chicago history, "it is when they visit the quiet and beautiful retreats of the suburbs, where thousands of its best citizens make their homes, that they are more

than surprised." North from Evanston, a line of wealthy suburbs evolved along the lake, including Wilmette (**FIGURE 102**). To the outsider they might have looked pretty much alike: big houses owned by the well-to-do near the lake, small business districts at the commuter railroad stations, and street after street of small cottages for the servant class west of the tracks. But members of elite families such as Arthur Meeker could make distinctions. "In our book Evanston was put down as pious and fuddy-duddy, with Wilmette and Kenilworth its twin daughters, who bore a fatal resemblance to their mother; Glencoe, frankly Jewish; Highland Park, not frankly ditto, and rather common as well; it was considered distinctly slumming to attend the dances at Exmoor Country Club. Winnetka was a little better."

Most prestigious of all was Lake Forest. "Too far from the loop for the convenience of any but

FIGURE 103. The Pullman Works, Pullman, ca. 1900.

the wealthy," noted John and Ruth Ashenhurst, "it maintains a studied aloofness in which it is aided by the deepest ravines, the highest walls, the thickest hedges and the largest building lots." By the 1950s, however, even Lake Forest had been pulled into Chicago's commuting orbit. Journalist James Morris observed what had become a daily ritual. "Each evening at Lake Forest," he wrote, "when the club train pulls in, a most cheerful and well-acquainted group of businessmen emerges from its cushioned recesses, and parts with fond expressions of fraternity." Having sat in swivel chairs, they stepped down onto the station platform with a glass of bourbon in one hand and a newspaper in the other. "There parked beside the line are the long polished rows of their limousines ..., a well-dressed wife ..., [and] a couple of poodles or a huge lugubrious mastiff peering through the back window."

CHICAGO'S INDUSTRIAL SATELLITES

Various small cities evolved peripheral to Chicago with a variety of industries such as clock- and watchmaking, milk processing, steel production, and railroad car manufacture. Pullman, in fact, was a totally planned city, the inspiration of George Pullman (**FIGURE 103**). Marshland around Lake Calumet south of Chicago was available and relatively inexpensive, and it was there that Pullman built his town, complete with industrial shops (where his own company began the actual manufacture of sleeping cars), rental housing for his employees, and stores to serve them, as well as churches, schools, and parks. Everything was carefully arranged, but also carefully controlled by Pullman, who considered himself the benevolent landlord. The economic depression of the 1890s, however, led to declining wages at the plant, and many of the employees were laid

FIGURE 104. East Fox Street, Aurora, ca. 1910.

off. Pullman steadily raised rents, determined to maintain profits. The railroad strike that followed, coordinated by Eugene V. Debs and his American Railroad Union, was put down violently once federal troops intervened on the pretext that the U.S. mails were being disrupted. Whereas the town had been an important tourist attraction before the strike, in its aftermath relatively few visitors bothered to come.

Aurora occupied both banks of the Fox River some thirty-five miles west of the Loop. It was a diverse manufacturing city, with many of its factories owned by Chicagoans (FIGURE 104). Aurora was the first city in Illinois to light its streets with electricity: electric arc lamps were hung on tall towers, casting a shimmering moonlight-like glow over the downtown after dark.

Elgin, also located on the Fox River, was similarly factory-oriented. Two of its local industries

rose to national prominence, making Elgin well-known across the nation in its own right. The Elgin National Watch Company made a specialty of accurate timekeeping. Its plant, a massive six-story red brick building with a tall tower, was the city's most impressive landmark. In Elgin's hinterland, as around East St. Louis in southern Illinois, were many dairy farms owned largely by German Americans. Elgin became the Midwest's leading market for milk; its Board of Trade oversaw the fresh milk supply in Chicago and supplied cream and cheese across much of the Midwest. The Borden Company, founded by Gail Borden, was a pioneer in the marketing of condensed milk. Pictured in FIGURE 105A is Grove Avenue in Elgin; at right in the image is a local business school.

Joliet, along the Des Plaines River, first prospered with the completion of the Illinois and Michigan Canal, and then with the arrival of sev-

FIGURE 105A. Grove Avenue, Elgin, ca. 1905.

FIGURE 105B. Chicago Street, Joliet, ca. 1905.

FIGURE 106. The Illinois State Penitentiary, Stateville, ca. 1925.

eral railroads: in turn, the Chicago and Alton; the Chicago, Rock Island and Pacific; and the Atchison, Topeka and Santa Fe. The motto "City of Steel" reflected the completion in 1869 of the Joliet Works, later also part of U.S. Steel. While construction of the canal and the railroads attracted large numbers of Irish immigrants, the steel mill attracted mainly eastern and southern Europeans, especially Poles and Italians. Industrial development also included coke plants, wire mills, a boiler works, a stove works, a horseshoe factory, machine shops, and an oil refinery. At one time or another, manufacturers in the city produced wallpaper, greeting cards, pianos, windmills, and corn shellers. Chicago's Hart, Schaffner and Marx clothing was also manufactured there. FIGURE 105B shows Joliet's main retail street. The eye is drawn to a distant vanishing point by the receding building facades, the power lines, and the streetcar tracks, all contributing to a heightened sense of perspective.

Joliet was known for limestone quarrying. A complex of prisons evolved in and around the city, built of the distinctive yellow stone, much of it quarried by the prisoners themselves. Joliet stone was used for the locks, aqueducts, and bridges along the Illinois and Michigan Canal. It was widely used in Chicago, for example on the waterworks on the city's north side. At Stateville, just north of Joliet, one of the nation's largest prisons was built (FIGURE 106), complete with a hospital, elementary, secondary, and vocational schools, and workshops for the making of furniture (with which state offices and college classrooms were furnished) and sundry other products, including motor vehicle license plates. Illinois's other main prison was at Chester in the far southern part of the state.

A city in itself, the Great Lakes Naval Station north of Lake Bluff was the largest naval training base in the United States, despite being far removed from both the Atlantic and the Pacific

FIGURE 107. The Great Lakes Naval Station, 1918.

Coast (**FIGURE 107**). And although it was situated on Lake Michigan, it did not have a harbor. Opened in 1911, the base played an important role in World War I, preparing some 50,000 sailors for duty. "All structures are of the most classic type, substantial and imposing by reason of their simplicity," reported one guidebook. "They are fireproof as construction warrants, steam-heated and lighted by electricity. The Administration Building with its tower reaching an altitude of 300 feet above the bluff, commands a wide view of the water from the east, and stretches of upland and prairie forest and dreamy woodlands to the west." Closed after World War I, the base was reactivated in 1935. It then trained over a million men and women, more than one-third of the personnel who served in the U.S. Navy during World War II. Between November 1, 1940, and June 30, 1945, some 235,000 Illinoisans served in the U.S. Navy, 38,000 in the

Marine Corps, and 10,000 in the Coast Guard. Some 616,000 Illinois residents served in the U.S. Army, including the Air Corps. During the war, 11.5 percent of the state's population was in uniform, compared with 9.2 percent nationwide. Located just south of Lake Forest, and also fronting on Lake Michigan, was the U.S. Army's Fort Sheridan.

WELCOMING THE FUTURE

After World War II, Chicago's suburban expansion continued, reaching westward, for example, as far as Elgin, Aurora, and Joliet by the end of the twentieth century. The maturation of air travel contributed, but it was primarily increased dependence on travel by car that underpinned metropolitan decentralization. Freeways radiated out from the Loop with a bypass tollway for motorists seeking to avoid the city center. The increased use of automobiles drastically impacted Chicago itself.

Streetcar thoroughfares were converted into auto-oriented commercial strips. Substantial real estate was taken for the new freeway, in swaths of land that fragmented many inner-city neighborhoods. At the very center, more than two-thirds of the Loop was dedicated to motor vehicles either moving or parked. Latter-day postcard art, however, pictured very few of the automobile's negative implications. Postcard publishers much preferred the traditional sorts of views popular from earlier years: bird's-eye views of skylines, vistas along downtown streets, and pictures of landmarks, especially things monumental. Traditional postcard iconography, in other words, continued to satisfy. But new airports and new highways could not be totally ignored, and they were not.

As Chicago's central location made it the nation's railroad hub, it also encouraged the city's rise in commercial aviation. In 1922, planners called for the creation of several "flying fields" around the city's periphery, but only one was built. Located on the city's southwest side, it was improved in the early 1930s as the Chicago Municipal Airport. Its name was changed to Midway Airport during World War II to honor those killed at the Battle of Midway. By 1945, the airport was handling some 1.3 million passengers a year; by 1956, that number had risen to 9 million. Midway's runways, however, proved too short for large jet aircraft. Orchard Field, located northwest of Chicago where the Douglas Aircraft Company had manufactured bombers during the war, was thus expanded as Midway's complement. Renamed Chicago O'Hare Airport in 1949 (to honor flying ace Edward O'Hare, who was killed in World War II), it quickly claimed the title of "world's busiest." "The most impressive first sight of the Midwest," wrote Graham Hutton, "is when you fly into Chicago at night from the East, descending over the blackness of the prairie to the great, ruddy blast furnaces and steel mills, catching the first winkings of the Lindbergh beacon from the Palmolive Building away on the starboard bow, and watching the brilliant rectangles formed by a thousand square miles of straight streets and buildings. Huge, sprawling city of swamp and prairie; one community of many communities, *communitas communitatum*." Numerous airlines, including industry giant United Airlines, have had their headquarters in Chicago over the years (FIGURE 108).

A new highway dramatically altered the city's lakefront. Lake Shore Drive evolved from a parkway into a freeway, with leisurely motoring giving way to hectic high-speed commuting. In the suburbs, auto use fostered sprawling urban development between the more densely built railroad corridors. Much of the metropolitan area's retailing moved to suburban shopping centers, and otherwise accumulated along suburban commercial strips. FIGURE 109 shows a section of the Illinois Tollway (also known as the "Tri-State") soon after it opened. With widely spaced interchanges, the road was originally intended as a bypass around Chicago. Within a decade, however, it also became flooded with commuters traveling from one suburban location to another as well as downtown. The caption on this postcard reads: "Scenic view along the Illinois Tollway. 187 miles of Super Tollway linking Chicago and northern Illinois to the nation's Tollway Network." From today's perspective, the almost total lack of traffic is somewhat disconcerting.

Increased automobile use fostered architectural innovation: for example, the shopping center was quickly followed by the shopping mall. The sale of goods and services directly to motorists led to new building forms: the gas station, the drive-in restaurant, and the motel. For retail businesses to thrive, they had to be automobile-convenient, if not fully automobile-oriented. The motel, which evolved after World War II out of the lowly tourist court, was originally an edge-of-city

FIGURE 108. Advertising postcard for United Airlines, ca. 1950.

FIGURE 109. The Illinois Tollway, ca. 1958.

FIGURE 110. Advertising postcard for the Shore Drive Motel, ca. 1960.

(or edge-of-town) affair. But by 1960, large hotel-like motor inns, such as the Shore Drive Motel pictured in FIGURE 110, had invaded city centers. The caption on this card states: "Beautifully located on the lake, yet only 12 minutes from the Loop. Delightful spacious rooms, free enclosed parking, free outdoor pool and gay sun-deck." The motel, wedged between tall apartment towers, was actually separated from the lake by six lanes of freeway traffic.

[ ]

Chicago offered postcard publishers a wealth of subject matter over the years, and the views they produced served to document the changes both in the city itself and in people's perceptions and expectations of it. But while the "mighty, monstrous, multifarious" metropolis may have been uppermost in most people's minds when they thought about Illinois, it was not the sum total of the state. From Galena in the north to Cairo in the south, from county seats to rural hamlets and their surrounding farms, there has always been more of Illinois worth showing. The great variety of postcards depicting the rest of the state have their own important stories to tell. And as integrally tied as Chicago was to the functioning of its hinterland, what one saw of Illinois beyond the Chicago metropolis fully reflected the metropolis itself.

PART TWO

Illinois beyond the Metropolis

FIGURE 111. Novelty postcard, ca. 1940.

The novelty card in FIGURE 111 says: "Greetings from Illinois." "Illinois" was a French adaptation of a term the Kaskaskia used in identifying themselves as "men." The Illinois Indians, once part of the Miami nation, were scattered up and down the Illinois River, the river's name being ultimately applied to the state. Many commentators have considered Illinois, including Chicago, to be

LOCK IN ILLINOIS RIVER AT HENRY, ILL.

FIGURE 112. The Illinois River, Henry, ca. 1900.

the most American of all the states. As journalist Clyde Davis observed: "It's the U.S.A. in a capsule. Here our virtues and our faults are most exaggerated and magnified. Here somehow the heroes seem more heroic, the villains more villainous, the buffoons more comic. Here violence is more unrestrained, and the capacity for greatness is as limitless as the sweep of the unending cornfields." "It is the heartland," wrote Donald Culross Peattie. Illinois "is core American," asserted David Steele; its prairie flatness was a slate upon which the nation's core values were expressed. Sherwood Anderson wrote:

> Back of Chicago the open fields—were you ever there?
> Trains coming toward you out of the West—
> Streaks of light on the long grey plains?—many a song—
> Aching to sing.

Pictured in **FIGURE 112** is the Illinois River near the Marshall County town of Henry. A lock is visible at the center of the image, part of the first lock and dam on the river, built just after the Civil War. The first bridge across the river was built here as well. A canal boat lies just off to the left; the Hennepin Canal was located just upriver, a connector to the Rock and Mississippi Rivers at Rock Island. In the 1930s, the Illinois River was improved with new locks and dams situated at intervals so as to maintain a nine-foot channel. Called the Illinois Waterway, it allowed barge traffic to move from the Mississippi River near Alton to Chicago by way of the Sanitary and Ship Canal, thus remaining an important route for moving grain, coal, limestone, and other bulk commodities. The reversal of the Chicago River, which sent pollutants from Chicago down the Illinois, negatively impacted the downriver fishery, which, when the photograph from which this postcard was made was taken, was second in the United States only to that of the Columbia River as a source of freshwater fish. What is beneficial to Chicago has not always been beneficial downstate (and vice versa), creating the grounds for political tension.

THE "LAND OF LINCOLN"

Abraham Lincoln was not an Illinoisan by birth, but he lived most of his adult life in the state, and it was his Illinois political career that led him to the White House as the sixteenth president of the United States. Wrote Illinois governor Henry Horner in 1939: "He was born in Kentucky; he attained his majority as a resident of Indiana; and the national capital saw the final flowering of his genius. Nevertheless, in his own time, he was Abraham Lincoln of Illinois, and so I believe he would have liked to be known as long as the American people revere his name." Thus Illinois has long been known as the "Land of Lincoln," a motto that eventually began appearing on state license plates in 1954 and was adopted as the official state slogan the following year.

The novelty card in FIGURE 113 honors Lincoln's "railsplitter" persona, an image rooted in the years he spent at New Salem, a pioneer community on the banks of the Sangamon River in Menard County, some twenty miles northwest of his eventual home in Springfield. Lincoln first became acquainted with New Salem when a flatboat he was piloting toward New Orleans snagged on the town's mill dam. He quickly returned to New Salem, his biographers tell us, where he split rails, tended store, became postmaster, ran unsuccessfully for elected office, became deputy county surveyor, and volunteered for the Blackhawk War. The village site was abandoned when Menard County was formed and the nearby town of Petersburg, its plat originally surveyed by Lincoln, was named the county seat. A century later, New

FIGURE 113. Lincoln commemorative postcard, 1916.

Salem was re-created as a state park: a shrine not only to Lincoln but to the American pioneering spirit. According to the caption on this postcard, the broad axe pictured here was owned by a resident of nearby Petersburg. The ox yoke, which was made by Lincoln, belonged to the University of Illinois. "It is kept in an oak cabinet in the rotunda of the Library Building," the caption tells us.

However, it is Springfield with which Lincoln is most closely associated. "Naturally, Springfield

FIGURE 114. Lincoln commemorative postcard, 1916.

born and one is buried." It was in Springfield that Lincoln was buried. And it was from that grave that some Springfield residents said his spirit continued to roam the town. As Vachel Lindsay penned:

> It is portentous, and a thing of state,
> That here at midnight, in our little town,
> A mourning figure walks, and will not rest,
>   Near the old court-house pacing up and
>   down.

Of course, Lincoln belonged not just to Illinois but to the nation, as the novelty card in FIGURE 114 suggests. While he was held in low esteem by many Americans while he was president, his great accomplishment in saving the Union, as well as his martyr's death, made him a national cult figure equal only to George Washington. After his death, most Americans, even southerners, came to appreciate his humanity. Wrote essayist Albert Woldman: "In reverent devotion his grateful countrymen began to weave around the memory of this superbly human man of the people a gossamer garment of appreciation and veneration, spun out of the filaments of wonder and hero-worship."

CITIES DOWNSTATE

Springfield

The distinctive meaning of a place was most readily symbolized in postcard art through the picturing of well-known local landmarks. Two of Springfield's landmark buildings are shown in FIGURE 115, its city hall on the left and, by far the most celebrated, the Lincoln house on the right. Donated to the state by Robert, the president's surviving son, the Lincoln home remains a place of pilgrimage for aficionados of American history. Although the original furnishings were taken to Chicago and were subsequently lost in the 1871 fire, the house was refurnished in the

is saturated with memory of Lincoln," Edgar Lee Masters emphasized. It was from Springfield that Lincoln practiced law out on the Eighth Judicial Circuit. It was from Springfield that he departed for Washington and the presidency. Lincoln himself said: "To this place and the kindness of these people I owe everything. Here I have lived a quarter of a century and have passed from a young man to an old man. Here my children have been

FIGURE 115. City Hall and the Lincoln family home, Springfield, ca. 1910.

fashion of Abraham and Mary Lincoln's time. The deceit proved highly convincing. "There is none of that aura of dry antiquity about Lincoln's home in Springfield," confided the editors of *Holiday*. "You really feel as if Abe and Mary and the boys had just stepped out and will be back in an hour or so. You can picture his lanky form on the haircloth sofa or working at his desk."

Especially interesting is the personal message written on this card. It reads in part: "Hellow! I am in the capitol of the Succor State Today." Of course, the word the writer needed was "sucker" rather than "succor." If the latter word had been accurate, Illinoisans might very well still be using the term today. Illinois was once known as the "Sucker State," just as neighboring Indiana was the "Hoosier State" and Wisconsin the "Badger State." Suckers were slow-moving bot-

tom fish. Suckers were also "born every minute." They included, for example, the settlers who had been "suckered" into buying what early in the nineteenth century was thought to be worthless prairie land.

The capitol building that Abraham Lincoln knew was located in Springfield's central square, across from the office that he shared with his law partner William Herndon. That building became the Sangamon County Courthouse. Attempts were made in the years immediately after the Civil War to move the capital, first to Chicago and then to Peoria, and finally to East St. Louis, of all places. But the completion in 1876 of the new capitol building in FIGURE 116 guaranteed that state government would stay in Springfield. The State of Illinois, of course, became the city's largest employer. And the annual session of the state legisla-

FIGURE 116. The Illinois State Capitol, Springfield, ca. 1930.

ture invigorated the city's hotel life, as well as its retail trade. Other important landmark structures were erected around the new capitol building, including the classically styled State Office Building and State Supreme Court Building.

Illinois was one of the leading farm states, so it comes as no surprise that it had one of the nation's largest state fairs. Begun at Springfield in 1851, the Illinois State Fair moved around from one year to the next, ranging as far north as Chicago and Sterling and as far south as Alton and Olney. In 1894, Springfield donated a large tract of land to the state for what would become a permanent fairgrounds. The Dome Building, which had stood at the center of the Court of Honor at the World's Columbian Exposition in Chicago, was disassembled and re-erected as the new facility's centerpiece. **FIGURE 117** depicts the racetrack with its large grandstand, showing spectators taking in a race between an automobile and an airplane. The photographer added to the sense

of visual excitement by carefully positioning the camera. The composition features a foreground of animated spectators, with the track in the middle ground and a distant background suggestive of the fairground's large expanse. The car on the track and the airplane overhead serve as clear focal points. Each year's fair featured a variety of attractions. As Edgar Lee Masters summed it up, "The event is attended by farmers from all parts of the state to see the display of stock and crops, to watch the races, and to hear the political haranguers who make the event an occasion to advance their pursuit of office."

Peoria

Peoria grew back from the Illinois River across a series of elevated terraces and up the steep valley bluffs. "From the Bluffs residential Peoria commands a view of the clustered business district, the serrated line of mills and factories along the curving river, and, far beyond the industrial sub-

Watching the races at the Illinois State Fair at Springfield from the porch of Sears, Roebuck and Co.'s Building.

FIGURE 117. The Illinois State Fairgrounds, Springfield, ca. 1910.

urbs [and to the east beyond], the checkered farm fields," wrote a state guidebook. Pictured in FIGURE 118 is the 1876 Peoria County Courthouse with its elaborate dome. Off to the right is the 1919 Peoria Life Insurance Building, its white terra-cotta cladding and pyramidal tower reminiscent of structures such as the Wrigley Building in Chicago.

Peoria's factories turned out plows, threshing machines, millwork, and washing machines. The city had the second-largest stockyard downstate, after National City near East St. Louis, which specialized in corn-fed hogs. It was also a distillery center. The city was ideally situated in the nation's Corn Belt, and it had abundant water and coal, both consumed in large quantities when corn whiskey was made. Mash, a distillery byproduct, found a ready market as animal feed. Peoria business interests organized the Distillers' and Cattle Feeders' Trust (the so-called "Whiskey Trust") in 1887, and briefly controlled the distilling industry

nationwide. During Prohibition, the city's distilleries turned to producing industrial alcohol, but they resumed whiskey production once Prohibition was repealed. Hiram Walker and Sons built the world's largest distillery along the riverfront.

Peoria's name derives from the Illinois tribe that once resided locally, but it came to symbolize American mainstream values. The phrase "Will it play in Peoria?" originated with vaudeville in a reference to popular tastes. Graham Hutton observed that there was "a definite if undefinable flavor to a Midwest city." But it was not, he said, so much a landscape thing as something associated directly with people. "While [American] cities may all look alike, it is the people who make the life and atmosphere of them; and the people are different. . . . To begin with, [in Midwestern cities] there is far more equality, individualism, elbow-thrusting, casualness, square-shoulderedness, slap-happiness, self-assurance, and self-assertion on the part of

FIGURE 118. Courthouse Square, Peoria, 1921.

the people you see in the depot or on the street. They are clearly less inhibited, and, as easterners say, they are also more unsophisticated." Then he added: "So much the worse for sophistication!"

The Holt Manufacturing Company of Stockton, California, opened a factory in Peoria to produce its "crawler tractor," a heavy machine with wheels that turned on paired link belts. After merging with a West Coast rival, the firm, renamed the Caterpillar Tractor Company, chose to locate its headquarters in Peoria, as it was central to the national market both for farm tractors and for construction equipment. Pictured in **FIGURE 119** is the quality control section of the company's main Peoria plant. Undergoing inspection are the diesel-powered tractors that became the company's stock and trade: the tractors one saw on literally every road-building project nationwide from the 1920s on. Internal combustion engines steadily replaced horsepower on midwestern farms. Tractors also continued to be manufactured in

Chicago, of course, with McCormick, Deering, and other firms merging early in the twentieth century to form International Harvester.

Rock Island and Moline

Along with Davenport, Iowa, located across the Mississippi River, and Moline, adjacent in Illinois, Rock Island was one of the "Tri-Cities" (today's "Quad Cities" with the addition of East Moline). Farm implement and other factories lined the river on either side of Rock Island's downtown, while back from the river, residential neighborhoods spread to, up, and across the top of the steep bluffs from which the photo used to produce the postcard in **FIGURE 120** was taken. In 1854, the Chicago and Rock Island Railroad (later the Chicago, Rock Island and Pacific) connected the city with Chicago some 150 miles to the east, and then built the first bridge across the Mississippi River, immediately extending its line to Omaha, some 300 miles west. Whereas large numbers of Irish and

FIGURE 119. The Caterpillar Tractor Company plant, Peoria, 1936.

FIGURE 120. Downtown Rock Island, ca. 1910.

FIGURE 121A. Advertising postcard for the Deere and Mansur Company, Moline, ca. 1905.

Germans dominated Peoria's working classes, at Rock Island, and also at Moline, Swedes were foremost. Rock Island was an important lumber center until the hardwood trees of the Mississippi River floodplain played out; it was where Frederick Weyerhaeuser, whose timber empire eventually extended to the Pacific Northwest, got his start.

Rock Island had a branch plant of Chicago's International Harvester Company, but Moline had the main plants for other sizeable firms, which eventually merged to form the Minneapolis-Moline Company and John Deere and Company. In the small northern Illinois town of Grand Detour, John Deere had perfected the self-scouring, steel-tipped plow. Traditional iron-tipped wooden plows had proved incapable of breaking the dense prairie sod, and incapable, as well, of shedding the sticky, gumbo-like prairie earth. Deere moved his plow works to Moline, where steel was more readily obtained, first by steamboat and then by railroad. Whereas Grand Detour remained a small

town, Moline, largely because of Deere and his various business partners, became a small city. The Deere and Mansur Company, whose plant is pictured in FIGURE 121A, originally made corn planters. In this view, stacks of wood stand in the open. Under roof were the millworks where lumber was cut and sized, the foundry where metal frames were forged, the splitting mill where metal sheets were cut and bent into shape, and the assembly lines where workers welded and bolted machines together. The Tri-City was also home to the Rock Island Arsenal, located on Arsenal Island, still the largest government-owned weapons-manufacturing complex in the United States. FIGURE 121B shows the Arsenal's equipment shop as it appeared in 1907.

Rockford

Factories lined the Rock River at Rockford in Winnebago County. In the view in FIGURE 122, an artist has reinforced the structural outlines of build-

FIGURE 121B. The Rock Island Arsenal, ca. 1910.

FIGURE 122. The Rock River, Rockford, ca. 1915.

FIGURE 123. The West Street business district, Rockford, ca. 1960.

ings and made every window shine brightly. The image suggests what might have been seen on a starry night. A Chamber of Commerce brochure celebrated Rockford's industrial successes: "Scattered here and there all over the great state of Illinois . . . are scores of live, hustling, wide-awake manufacturing cities whose shops and factories are humming with activity and whose products are known the world around. Among these cities . . . Rockford takes first rank, with the single city of Chicago removed from the equation." "Its knitting mills send out each year more hosiery than is produced by any other city in the world." The city was a leader in the manufacture of leather goods and locks. And if one wanted to get down to the details, it was also a leader in the manufacture of horse collars, fly nets, and hog troughs. It was "famed for its beautiful streets, its magnificent houses, its extensive park and playground

system, its drives and its boulevards, and blessed by a magnificent foliage, which has earned for it the title 'Forest City,'" the brochure said. As in Rock Island and Moline, the largest immigrant group in Rockford was from Sweden.

Located some eighty-five miles west of Chicago, Rockford was divided by the Rock River. Laid out on a series of street grids, each oriented differently to the meandering river, the city had several business districts. The largest, depicted in FIGURE 123, evolved just west of the ford in the river that early gave the city its name. But it was in the business area immediately to the east that the city's largest department store and largest hotel were built in the early twentieth century. A mile southeast from there, another commercial zone evolved, oriented to the city's large Swedish-speaking population, a neighborhood of factory workers largely dependent upon employment at the National Lock

U. S. 309. Bloomington, Ill. McLean County Court House.

FIGURE 124. The McLean County Courthouse, Bloomington, ca. 1910.

Company and J. H. Manny and Company (later J. L. Case), another farm implement manufacturer. By the 1960s, retailers in all three business districts were feeling the competition of suburban shopping centers. The improved street lighting downtown, as pictured here, was one result.

Bloomington-Normal

Bloomington, too, had its factories, as well as the shops of the Chicago and Alton Railroad. Several large insurance companies were also located there, including today's giant State Farm Insurance Company. The McLean County Courthouse, shown in **FIGURE 124**, opened in 1900 but was substantially rebuilt following a fire a few months later that devastated much of Bloomington's downtown. McLean is the state's largest county geographically and has long been the state's leading agricultural county in terms of farm output.

This postcard was mailed on a Saturday in 1919. The message concerns an intended ride to town the next day by electric interurban car. "I wrote you a letter telling you I would be in town Sunday on the quarter to 9 car, but that makes me hurry so much that [I] will come later . . . on the quarter to 11 . . . meet me . . . and I will take you to church." Today, most Americans forget (if they ever knew) how fast and how dependable the U.S. Postal Service once was. In many localities, postcards could be used to set and change appointments, even within the course of a few hours' time. Streetcars carried mailboxes, which were emptied after every run. In many cities, mail was delivered to homes several times a day.

FIGURE 125 shows Bloomington's Courthouse Square immediately after the 1900 fire. The pictured aftermath of a fire, flood, or tornado sold many postcards over the years, the card with this

5506. Business Section of Bloomington, Ill., after the fire of June, 1900.

FIGURE 125. Courthouse Square, Bloomington, 1900.

particular view having been mailed in 1911. Harold Sinclair, in his novel *Years of Illusion*, described the night downtown Bloomington went up in flames. Clerks in the courthouse and lawyers in offices up above stores rushed to bundle up business records and other valuables. For the novel's hero, it was of little avail. "When he had hoisted the bundle to a shoulder he paused for a moment, taking what might be a last look around the dingy office which had served both his father and grandfather. They had sat ... at these tables and desks, planned this and that in these rooms." Others, however, retreated to the safety of distant taverns. "They Goddamned and by-Godded and fished in their pockets for more silver to buy more drinks or stood morose and silent over their glasses while behind them the holocaust roared on."

Originally just another courthouse town with dirt streets and prairie grasses pushing in all around, Bloomington saw its fortunes change dramatically in the 1850s with the arrival of the Chicago and Alton Railroad. Located roughly halfway between Chicago and St. Louis, Bloomington was a logical location for the company's repair shops, where locomotives were torn down and put back together again and fully refitted. (**FIGURE 126**). It was here that George Pullman first contracted to have his sleeping cars built. Here also was where the nation's first dining cars were manufactured. Besides railroading and insurance, Bloomington was a leader in hybrid corn production; the large Funk Brothers Seed Company, for example, was headquartered in the city. The Funk family was one of Illinois's largest landowners. Indeed, much of central Illinois was originally owned in parcels of approximately 20,000 acres in size, with the poorly drained land used originally for cattle ranching. Prime among those landowners was

FIGURE 126. The Chicago and Alton railroad shops, Bloomington, ca. 1910.

Samuel Allerton, a founder of Chicago's Union Stock Yards, promoter of the first belt railroad around the city, and an investor in the First National Bank, long Chicago's largest.

Jesse Fell, little known to Americans today, influenced national politics as few men have either before or since. He established Illinois State Normal University, whose original "Old Main" is pictured in FIGURE 127. Normal, Bloomington's smaller sister city, was named for the college. More importantly, it was Fell who nominated Abraham Lincoln for the U.S. Senate in 1858, and who engineered the debates between Lincoln and Stephen A. Douglas, the Senate incumbent, that brought Lincoln to national prominence. It was Fell who persuaded Lincoln to write a short autobiography, which Fell then published and subsequently distributed across the nation shortly before the 1860 Republican National Conven-

tion in Chicago. It was Fell, along with his former law partner Judge David Davis, who engineered Lincoln's victory at that convention. Among the promotional tactics employed was the parading by Lincoln supporters of split rails through the Chicago streets. Lincoln would not have become president without Jesse Fell.

Now known as Illinois State University, the institution functioned through most of its history primarily as a place to teach teachers to teach. "It requires only a registration fee of thirty dollars for students pledging themselves to teach in Illinois," explained a state historical guide. "Its courses comprise a two year junior college course for teachers of elementary schools, and a four year course leading to a degree of Bachelor of Education." Among the earliest of the nation's normal schools, the college was part of the national movement for free public education launched by Horace Mann. To ob-

FIGURE 127. Illinois State Normal University, Normal, 1910.

tain the university, Bloomington-Normal success-fully edged out Peoria and Batavia, the latter place located on the Fox River midway between Aurora and Elgin. Other normal schools were established at Carbondale (today's Southern Illinois Universi-ty), Charleston (today's Eastern Illinois University), DeKalb (today's Northern Illinois University), and Macomb (today's Western Illinois University).

Champaign-Urbana

Disaster strikes in downtown Champaign, and a postcard photographer, whose studio is only a few doors away, is there. That city's "million dollar fire" took place on St. Patrick's Day, 1915 (FIGURE 128). Like Bloomington and Normal, some forty miles to the northwest, Champaign is twinned with adjacent Urbana. Since 1869, the campus of the University of Illinois has straddled the corporate line that divides the two municipalities. Urbana was founded in the 1830s, the seat of Champaign County, McLean County's arch-competitor for the

title of Illinois's leading farm producer. When in the 1850s the "Chicago branch" of the Illinois Cen-tral Railroad was run two miles to the west, the separate and ultimately larger municipality of Champaign emerged. As in McLean County, the coming of a railroad, coupled with state legisla-tion legalizing drainage districts as taxing units, along with new drainage technologies such as dredge boats and drainage tile, fostered conver-sion of the area's wet prairies from cattle grazing to crop cultivation.

Champaign and Urbana developed their own individual personalities. "Although not an indus-trial town," reported a state guidebook, "Cham-paign is the worldlier of the two, with its railroads, its bustling business district, and its 20-odd fac-tories that manufacture [drainage] tiles, concrete mixers, gloves, soy bean products, and a dozen others. Urbana, which is heavily wooded, gives the impression of being more leisurely and maintains that subdued dignity characteristic of a Midwest

FIGURE 128. Fire on South Neil Street, Champaign, 1915.

county seat." The role of the University of Illinois (originally the Illinois State Industrial University) was to prepare students for careers in agriculture and engineering. Extensive farm experiment fields, including what is today the nation's oldest, dominated Urbana's south side.

The railroad station was a community's front door. It was there that people caught their first glimpse of a city or had their last look at it. It was at the station that telegrams were received and sent, and packages as well. Before widespread use of the telephone and the radio, news of the outside world usually arrived at the local train station first. And it was there that candidates for important public offices appeared, often leaving very quickly in order to make a stop at another railroad station in another town or city farther down the line. In **FIGURE 129**, President William Howard Taft is addressing a crowd in Champaign

from the back of a campaign train. Although the photo is well composed, it is nonetheless an amateur's snapshot, most likely taken with a hand-held camera.

"Search for the average farmer or shopkeeper in Illinois and you'll find a parent with a son or daughter at the University of Illinois, Northwestern University in Evanston, the progressive University of Chicago, or in one of the two dozen other colleges the state contains," marveled one visitor to the state. Nonetheless, whereas the sons and daughters of affluent parents (not just from Illinois, but from across the nation) made their way to Chicago's prestigious private universities, the families who patronized the University of Illinois tended more to the middle classes (and came mainly from within the state). A large proportion of the university's students were the first generation within their families to attend college.

FIGURE 129. President William Howard Taft's campaign train, Champaign, 1912.

Favoring agriculture, engineering, and eventually the hard sciences, the University of Illinois was rooted in midwestern utilitarianism. It was one of the nation's sixty-eight institutions of higher education formed under the Morrill Land Grant Act, which was proposed by Jonathan Baldwin Turner, a professor at Illinois College in Jacksonville, and signed into law by Abraham Lincoln in 1862. "To a visitor there is something outlandish about the size and setup of the University of Illinois," wrote Ann Carnahan. "He will be too numb for comment when he hears the student band that plays at the big intercollegiate football games is about half as large as the entire Princeton undergraduate class." "When the bell rings on this Midwest campus," she added, "thousands of students swarm like ants on a burning log." The class of 1914 is pictured in FIGURE 130. They are lined up in front of Altgeld Hall, named for Governor John P. Altgeld,

whose support of labor during the Pullman Strike cost him reelection. In 1914, the university was the third-largest in the United States.

Viewer beware! One cannot believe everything that is pictured or in print. Take a careful look at FIGURE 131. The caption on this postcard identifies the stadium's location as Chicago. (Was the assumption made that everything important in Illinois was necessarily in Chicago?) Furthermore, dubbed in is a lake with mountains in the distance—geographical features of which, in this flat Corn Belt landscape, there are few and none, respectively. This stadium, built as a memorial to the graduates of the University of Illinois who were killed in World War I, was in fact very much a part of the Champaign-Urbana scene. Among those who played in it was Harold E. Grange—the "Wheaton Iceman," the "Galloping Ghost"—whose antics on the football field became legend.

FIGURE 130. Senior class photo, University of Illinois, Urbana, 1914.

FIGURE 131. Memorial Stadium, University of Illinois, Champaign, ca. 1930.

Library, University of Illinois.—37

FIGURE 132. Main Library, University of Illinois, Champaign, ca. 1930.

"Red" Grange went on to play for the Chicago Bears, bringing the newly formed National Football League into public prominence.

In the 1920s, a plan formulated by society architect Charles Platt envisioned a significantly enlarged campus for the University of Illinois, to be formally organized around several large quadrangles intermixed with smaller, more intimate courtyards. The quadrangle idea was inspired by campus designs elsewhere, including Thomas Jefferson's plan for the University of Virginia. But it was also inspired by the Court of Honor at the 1893 World's Columbian Exposition, and accordingly remains a clear example of architectural Chicago's downstate reach. The Depression and then World War II brought campus growth to a temporary halt, however, and only a half-dozen of Platt's neo-Georgian buildings were completed, including the library pictured in FIGURE 132. It is still ranked as the fifth-largest university library in the nation, and the largest of any state univer-

sity. Although today's catalog contains more than 10 million items, there are no postcards listed. Only a handful of books are concerned with the history and the present-day uses of postcard art.

Decatur

Home to the shops of the Wabash Railroad, Decatur, in Macon County, like nearby Bloomington, was a railroader's town. "The northeast section of the city is a welter of tracks bordered by roundhouses where locomotives are periodically dismantled and refurbished, and by shops where coaches are overhauled," reported the Federal Writers' Project. "And yet Decatur is not a 'factory' town," it added, "although its 12,000 workers fabricate products ranging from fly swatters to steel bridges. Neither is it essentially a college town, despite its Millikin University, nor a farm town, although it is hedged in by a limitless stretch of farms in all directions. In part it is all of these." At bottom, Decatur was a "prairie city." "Prairie grass-

FIGURE 133. Lincoln Square, Decatur, 1932.

es and flowers push against the doorsteps of the outermost houses, and each spring brighten the vacant lots." Decatur's Lincoln Square is shown in FIGURE 133; the Transfer House, in the foreground, was built to shelter streetcar riders coming and going downtown.

Decatur labeled itself "Soy City" and claimed to be "the soybean capital of the world." Research at the University of Illinois (indeed, in the very building where these words are being written) resulted in soybean varieties that were well suited to the Midwest's Corn Belt climate. Decatur's A. E. Staley Manufacturing Company and its rival, Archer-Daniels-Midland, became the nation's largest soybean processors. FIGURE 134 shows the Staley industrial complex in about 1940. A substantial amount of farm acreage in east-central Illinois was given over to soybeans, in rotation with corn, of course. A strictly "cash grain" farm

economy came to dominate central Illinois in the east; the traditional feeding of corn to hogs, however, remained important to the west. Removed from the farm landscape were the Osage orange hedgerows and other fence lines that had once outlined farm fields. Most of the barns and other farmstead features that catered to animals had been demolished. In their place came metal storage bins, which allowed farmers to store their harvested grain in anticipation of higher commodity prices. Cash grain farmers not only farmed, they also played the futures market.

East St. Louis

Although East St. Louis was thought of as a factory city, it actually functioned primarily as a bedroom community for St. Louis, Missouri. Its residents worked mainly outside the city, for example, at the stockyard in nearby National City,

FIGURE 134. The A. E. Staley Manufacturing Company, Decatur, ca. 1940.

at the steel mill and enameling plant in nearby Granite City, or at the oil refinery near Wood River, none of which contributed to the East St. Louis tax base. Companies, in fact, organized their own municipalities—towns largely without residents—in order to keep their property taxes low, as well as to reduce the impact of zoning and other land-use controls. The result was an environment of dust, dirt, smoke, fumes, stockyard odors, and noise. With many antiquated factories closing after World War II, the area grew notorious for its landscape of blight and discard as well as environmental abuse. Nonetheless, early in the twentieth century, the city's downtown could impress (**FIG-URE 135**). The industrial conurbation centered in East St. Louis sprawled across the western parts of St. Clair and Madison Counties.

Automobile ownership allowed East St. Louis's more affluent residents to move to nearby Bel-leville, Collinsville, or Edwardsville, all located to the east on higher ground well above the Mississippi River floodplain. African Americans in East St. Louis, on the other hand, were confined residentially to the lowest sections of the city nearest the river and the city's railroad yards. "Negroes have their own schools, churches, grocery stores, and motion picture theaters," reported a state historical guide. "Industrial plants have begrimed the section; its sole strip of green is Lincoln Park. . . . An intermixed Negro and foreign born population lives in the 'Bad Lands' along Missouri Avenue . . . while the remnant of a once-sizeable Armenian colony dwells near 16th Street and Broadway." Bel-leville was centered on a large German American farming district given over mainly to dairying, a part of the St. Louis milkshed.

East St. Louis was laid out on a floodplain: the "American Bottoms," so named in the years before

FIGURE 135. Collinsville Avenue, East St. Louis, ca. 1905.

the Louisiana Purchase when Spain controlled the river's west bank and the new United States the east. In 1903, flood waters covered more than a quarter of the city, displacing over 8,000 residents (see figure 5). In anticipation of future floods, many of the streets at the city's center were graded up some eight or ten feet, with the new commercial buildings built on correspondingly high foundations. Where no buildings were erected, deep depressions remained. "Vacant lots along side streets resemble shallow quarry pits and the roofs of houses that antedate elevation of the streets are but a few feet higher than the pavement."

Alton

Alton, in far northwestern Madison County, was also located along the Mississippi River, but it was situated on the first high ground in Illinois upriver from St. Louis, thus just above the mouth of the

Missouri River and just below the mouth of the Illinois River. Early in the nineteenth century, Illinoisans thought that Alton would surely match St. Louis's growth. It was to Alton that the Illinois legislature first chartered the Chicago and Alton Railroad, although once the line was completed, it was quickly extended to St. Louis. Alton became little more than an economic satellite of its larger neighbor, a small city specializing in flour milling, explosives (for southern Illinois coal mines), and chemical production. FIGURE 136 shows the Alton waterfront with City Hall and the city's main railroad station. At the left, an electric interurban car waits at the ready. Houses in Alton spread up across the higher ground. "Residential Alton lies chiefly . . . on the bluffs," reported a state guidebook. "Here the expression 'going downtown' has literal meaning, for the streets that run to the river drop abruptly on a steep grade from im-

Railroad Depot and City Hall, Alton, Ill.

FIGURE 136. The Waterfront, Alton, ca. 1915.

mediately above the business district." It was at Alton that Elijah Lovejoy, the abolitionist newspaper editor, was murdered by a mob in 1837. In 1858, Abraham Lincoln and Stephen A. Douglas met in Alton for their last debate.

Quincy

Located farther up the Mississippi River, some seventy-five miles from Alton, Quincy became western Illinois's principal trade center, a strong competitor in the mid-nineteenth century with Peoria and Rockford, and even Galena, to be the state's second-largest city. Settled initially by New Englanders, the city was named for John Quincy Adams. It remains the seat of Adams County. German Americans dominated Quincy's economic and cultural life, and most of the city's buildings, as at Belleville, were accordingly built of red brick, German immigrants preferring masonry over wood frame construction. In the 1920s, a booster

brochure described the typical Quincy worker: "This workman spends the major portion of his time erecting pumps and compressors, building poultry and agricultural products, casting and mounting stoves, making metal wheels, compounding dyes, building freight and passenger elevators, making showcases and store fixtures, and producing strawboard and varieties of chip." "This Quincy workman," it added, "occupies 9,500 homes of which 65 per cent are owned by occupants. . . . He supports four building and loan associations." The postcard in FIGURE 137 offers a view over Quincy's downtown captured in 1905.

FIGURE 138 shows an excursion boat loading passengers, with everyone dressed in their Sunday best. The steamer in this postcard view is a reminder that the Mississippi River once had a viable steamboat trade. Through the nineteenth century, Quincy was an important shipping point on the river for wheat, corn, and pork. However,

FIGURE 137. Downtown Quincy, 1905.

FIGURE 138. The Waterfront, Quincy, 1908.

Entrance C., B. & Q. Wagon and
Railway Bridge, Quincy, Ill.

76-49

FIGURE 139. Chicago, Burlington and Quincy railroad bridge, Quincy, ca. 1915.

steamboats ran only seasonally, while railroads operated year-round. Whereas railroad cars could be added to and subtracted from trains to meet freight requirements, steamboats had a set freight-handling capacity and could not be so adjusted. Railroad trains were fast; steamboats were slow. For a number of reasons, the railroads won out, and the waterfronts of river towns such as Quincy were given over largely to railroading. This image shows warehouses, elevated on a river terrace, lining the waterfront; rail cars stand on sidings nearby.

Quincy was a western terminus for the early Chicago, Burlington and Quincy Railroad. The line was part of the strategy whereby Chicago commercial interests successfully diverted the trade of the Upper Mississippi Valley away from St. Louis, with commodities that had once gone south down the river going east by rail instead.

In the railroad era, river cities, to the extent that they continued to thrive, did so primarily as river-crossing places. It was the railroad bridge (FIGURE 139), in other words, and not the river landing, that counted. However, it was not from Quincy but from Burlington, located some sixty miles farther upriver on the Iowa side of the Mississippi, that a bridge carried the railroad's mainline westward to Omaha and then to Denver. Although the railroad was nicknamed "the Burlington Line," Quincy residents persisted in calling it "the Q."

As Quincy turned its back on the river, so too did it ultimately turn its back on the railroad, and indeed on downtown. Suburban shopping centers, including the one pictured in FIGURE 140, siphoned away the bulk of the city's retail trade. Unlike traditional business districts, which were compactly built, with multistory buildings elbowing one another close to streets and sidewalks, the

FIGURE 140. The Eastside Shopping Center, Quincy, ca. 1955.

new shopping districts were spread out: commercial strips with low, single-story buildings surrounded by parking lots, and thus well separated from one another. It was a whole new way of doing business, one that was convenient for motorists. And it was a whole new way of configuring cities. By and large, postcard publishers were not attracted to the nation's new roadsides. For one thing, the new cityscapes were visually stretched out. Largely lacking in verticality, they were not easily photographed. It was mainly in advertising cards such as this that roadside scenes got pictured.

Danville

Danville's downtown also centered on a courthouse square (FIGURE 141). The Vermilion County Courthouse faced the square on the east, across from which was the tower of the First National Bank. Although such office buildings were modest by Chicago standards, they clearly symbolized a city's commercial prowess. Danville was a coal-mining, glass-making, and grain-milling town. It was also home to the shops of the Chicago and Eastern Illinois Railroad—the bridge line that gave Chicago the most direct rail connections to both the American Southwest and the American Southeast. The nation's first strip mining for coal was conducted at Danville. Dredges that were normally used to dig drainage ditches across the area's wet prairies were turned instead to digging coal where it outcropped along the Vermilion River. Immigrants from Italy worked the mines, and immigrants from Belgium worked in the glass factories, but most of the city's residents were migrants from the Upper South. This postcard was addressed to "Mrs. Mattie Crain, Horse Cave, Kentucky, Hart County." Its message began:

FIGURE 141. Downtown Danville, 1922.

"Dearest Mama. I am sorry to hear you are sick." It was signed "Annie."

Trees were few in downtown business districts. Out in the residential areas of a city, however, tree canopies overspread the streets, bringing a suggestion of the picturesque to even the most regular of street grids. Along with the landscaped front yards of houses, trees symbolically transferred a kind of rural pastoralism to the city. Danville's premier residential thoroughfare, North Vermilion Street, is shown in **FIGURE 142**, along which the city's business elite built large houses. On this street lived Joseph Gurney "Uncle Joe" Cannon, who was elected to Congress in 1873 and served, save for four years, continuously until 1923. For ten years he was speaker of the House of Representatives. An intractable personality, he was, critics said, the archetypal "Standpat Republican." In a sense, the trees along North Vermilion Street died with Cannon. After his death, his house, pictured on the left, was torn down and replaced by Dan-

ville's first supermarket. The thoroughfare quickly unraveled as a residential place, eventually becoming a commercial strip.

Jacksonville

Factory employment tended to separate cities from towns. Public institutions also figured in the mix. Having lost its bid to be the state capital and having failed to secure the University of Illinois, Jacksonville in Morgan County did succeed in obtaining a large state hospital for the mentally ill and two state schools, one for the blind and the other for the deaf. The mental hospital, its main building begun in 1873, is pictured in **FIGURE 143A**. Additionally, Jacksonville had two private liberal arts colleges, Illinois College and MacMurray College. Two national political figures, Stephen A. Douglas and William Jennings Bryan, began their law practices in Jacksonville. The city's emphasis on education and public health reflected the origins of its earliest settlers, who were mainly

FIGURE 142. North Vermilion Street, Danville, ca. 1910.

FIGURE 143A. Jacksonville State Hospital, ca. 1920.

FIGURE 143B. The south side of Jacksonville Square, ca. 1905.

well-educated New Englanders. Jacksonville's downtown was vibrant, although FIGURE 143B shows it on what appears to have been a very quiet night. The arch at left, with its electric incandescent lamps, was common in small towns; local booster clubs and chambers of commerce tended to copy one another in establishing main street "white way" lighting.

Galesburg

Founded as a farm town by Presbyterian fundamentalists from New York, Galesburg in Knox County quickly evolved as a railroad center. It was from Galesburg that the Chicago, Burlington and Quincy Railroad branched to Burlington and Quincy. The line's principal repair shops were accordingly located there. Swedish immigrants were attracted to jobs in the city, including the family of the poet Carl Sandburg, whose father was a long-time employee of the Burlington Line. FIGURE 144 shows "Old Main" on the Knox College campus, the only Lincoln-Douglas debate site to retain its original character. Abraham Lincoln received an honorary degree from the college in 1860. Carl Sandburg attended school there, as did Edgar Lee Masters. In Galesburg, "Swedes and Calvinism prevailed," Masters remembered. "There you look at the prairie from railroad shops," he continued. "Galesburg is as different from Springfield, from the culture of New Salem, as Oslo is different from the Romantic Rhine, or Brittany, or Wessex. It is altogether different from Peoria; for in truth Illinois has sections of life, of human psychology, even as it has river lands, uplands, prairies and woodlands."

FIGURE 144. "Old Main," Knox College, Galesburg, ca. 1950.

ILLINOIS SMALL TOWNS

Americans were adopting big-city ways more and more, even in small towns and on farms. Nonetheless, many small-town and rural values persisted, even among those who moved to big cities. The agricultural frontier of the nineteenth century had fostered a distinctive American "idealism, optimism, materialism, and an abiding faith in progress," wrote historian Lewis Atherton. And it was in the nation's small towns, and especially those of the Midwest, he asserted, that such values were thought to center. As the economist Thorstein Veblen wrote: "The country town is one of the great American institutions; perhaps the greatest, in the sense that it has had and continues to have a greater part than any other in shaping public sentiment and giving character to American culture." Nonetheless, cities exerted a far greater influence as the twentieth century unfolded. Americans,

Illinoisans included, were now leaving family farms to go directly into factory jobs; small towns were no longer stepping-stones to the city. And like the nation's farmers, small-towners were increasingly viewed as parochial. Chicagoans were not alone in looking down on their "country cousins"; it was happening everywhere.

Postcard publishers treated the small town in a variety of ways. The images on postcards produced by local photographers for a largely local market tended to celebrate the "smiling aspects" of small-town life. As Theodore Dreiser marveled, "Walk into any drug or book store of any up to date small town today, and you will find in a trice nearly every scene of importance and really learn the character and charms of the vicinity." Publishers tended to seek out views that mimicked those of the big city: bird's-eye views, vistas along crowded streets, and views of monumental architecture,

FIGURE 145. Novelty postcard, ca. 1905.

for example. But the small town was frequently captured through the lens of negative stereotype, a teasing that even its residents could engage in. **FIGURE 145** features a cartoon image of the proverbial "one-horse town." The sender could write in the name of the place being visited and mail it off, providing entertainment for friends and relatives.

Washington Street in Macoupin County's Bunker Hill is shown in **FIGURE 146**. A typical midwestern main street, it had yet to be paved and otherwise upgraded when this photo was taken around 1905. Here farm families came to "trade," especially farm wives with their surplus butter, vegetables, and fruit. "The word lingers, though its meaning has been forgotten," novelist Rose Wilder Lane observed. "Americans who never bartered eggs for calico will say, 'I trade at So-and-So's,' or, 'He gets my trade.'" Barter was slowly supplanted by a cash economy in the decades after

the Civil War. Along the Midwest's main streets, stores pressed closely together. It was a pedestrian world. Once a farmer tied up his horses, he and his wife walked from store to store. Business activities inside were related by a simple formula to the public way outside. Buildings were long, narrow, rectangular boxes of one, two, or three stories, with one of the narrow ends facing the street. Signs and display windows helped draw customers inside, where sales space was invariably organized perpendicular to the street. Customers could find goods stacked on shelves along each wall, with clerks behind counters waiting to serve. Offices, apartments, or sometimes just storage rooms were located on upper floors. There might also be a large meeting room upstairs if the building was a lodge hall or an "opera house."

The more successful towns were those that had a factory or two, a mine, or some other source of

FIGURE 146. Washington Street, Bunker Hill, 1905.

industrial employment. A courthouse was particularly helpful. "A county seat town was tremendously important," the novelist Homer Croy observed. "Its lots sold for more than lots in jackleg towns; the laws were made there and the taxes assessed and the political plums handed out." Farmers who had business to do at a courthouse usually patronized nearby merchants, as did the county government itself. The majority of Illinois's 102 county seats had business districts organized around courthouse squares rather than along a single commercial main street. Around the sides of the typical square, wrote Graham Hutton, were located "the bank or banks, a battery of lawyers' offices ... two or three drug stores, some taverns, barber shops and at least one beauty parlor, doctors', dentists', and veterinaries' offices, the newspaper, and the usual array of hardware, clothing, and other stores."

Illinois's towns, like its cities, scaled down from large to small in hierarchical fashion. In 1920, for example, there were 20 towns with between 7,000 and 15,000 residents, 121 with 2,000 to 5,000, and 398 with 400 to 1,000. But the villages and hamlets with fewer than 400 residents were the most numerous of all, numbering more than 1,400. In 1920, retail functions had already begun to shift up the urban hierarchy, a result of the increased use of automobiles. The courthouse square at Monmouth, the seat of Warren County, is pictured in FIGURE 147, the automobile rather than the horse and wagon clearly dominant. The square was where a town's rituals took place, especially on ceremonial occasions such as the Fourth of July or Labor Day. It was on the courthouse lawn that historical events and persons important to the community were remembered on plaques. At Monmouth, one such marker honored native son Wyatt Earp.

Monmouth Public Square and Court House, Monmouth, Ill.—11

FIGURE 147. Courthouse Square, Monmouth, ca. 1925.

The courthouse at Lincoln stands boldly silhouetted in **FIGURE 148**. The seat of Logan County, Lincoln, Illinois, is the only place in the United States that was named for Abraham Lincoln with his knowledge and consent. It was to Lincoln's law office in Springfield that speculators, in anticipation of the arrival of the Chicago and Alton Railroad, went to draw up the legal papers requisite to establishing a new town. At the suggestion that the town be named for him, Lincoln is said to have replied: "All right, boys, go ahead, but I think you are making a mistake. I never knew anything named Lincoln that amounted to much." Logan County's first courthouse, part of the Eighth Circuit, which Lincoln attended as a lawyer, was located nearby at Postville (now part of the town of Lincoln). In the 1920s, the building was bought by Henry Ford and moved to his outdoor museum at Greenfield Village in Dearborn, Michigan, near Detroit. A replica of the courthouse was subsequently erected at the Postville site as a histori-

cal museum. Ford reportedly considered history to be "bunk." What he later said he meant was that written history was bunk. His kind of historicism resided in material culture, especially that of rural America, which the use of his Model T was threatening with extinction.

Climb a water tower, as did the photographer who captured the image on which **FIGURE 149** is based, and the typical small town spread out below. And with a community such as Savanna, in Carroll County, one did not have to linger long: the place could be seen in a glance or two. Small towns were, after all, small. The Mississippi River was never bridged at Savanna, but the town was located on the mainline of the Burlington Railroad, which connected Chicago with Minneapolis and St. Paul. Pictured here is the growth edge of Savanna, where stylish houses were being built. Symbolized in this view, perhaps, is a certain small-town smugness, or maybe a kind of regional contentment. In musing about Illinois's small

Logan County Court House
Lincoln, Illinois

FIGURE 148. The Logan County Courthouse, Lincoln, ca. 1925.

FIGURE 149. Savanna, ca. 1910.

FIGURE 150. Railroad station, Savanna, ca. 1915.

towns, Graham Hutton concluded: "Much of the shape, layout, compactness, communal solidarity, and social familiarity of Lincoln's Springfield still fills these rural towns of the Midwest." As a river town, Savanna spread up the river bluff, its streets on the terrace and floodplain below deflected to parallel the riverbank. Most Illinois small towns were on flat topography and were laid out, accordingly, on uninterrupted, rectilinear street grids.

Savanna may have been a river town, but on most days its largest crowds assembled not at the levee but at the railroad station. In **FIGURE 150** a number of people are awaiting a Chicago-bound passenger train. Yet it is an automobile that the photographer has placed front and center. Perhaps a local family was starting out on an afternoon's drive into the country. Initially considered a luxury—a plaything for the affluent—automobiles quickly became a middle-class, and then a working-class, necessity. Here a luxury car with one of the town's more affluent families is cross-

ing the tracks. After 1910, the farmers of the Middle West, especially of the Corn Belt, eagerly adopted motor cars and trucks, and for that matter, also farm tractors powered by internal combustion engines. Midwesterners represented Henry Ford's prime market for his Model T.

Blessed was the town with two railroads—or, as in San Jose, on the border of Logan and Menard Counties, two branch lines of a single railroad company, in this case the Chicago and Alton (**FIGURE 151**). Railroads competed with one another territorially. Depots were located at regular five- or six-mile intervals, and then streets were laid out, town lots were surveyed, and property was sold, often by the railroad company itself, or by a subsidiary. The idea was to establish narrow trade hinterlands perpendicular to each rail line and running back ten or eleven miles, the limit from which farmers could haul crops to town by wagon and return in a day. An overly dense railroad network was established in Illinois; thus, too many

C. & A. Bridge, San Jose, Ill.

FIGURE 151. Railroad junction at San Jose, ca. 1905.

small towns were created as well, a situation that became all too evident once the automobile arrived, precipitating a shift of central-place functions up the state's urban hierarchy. San Jose was largely a bedroom community by the 1960s, with most residents working and shopping in nearby Lincoln. It might very well have been San Jose that Mary Hartwell Catherwood described in her novel *The Spirit of an Illinois Town*: "The prairie was intersected by two railroads, and at their junction, without a single natural advantage, the town sprang up. Neither lake nor stream, neither old woods nor diversity of hills, lured man's enterprise to the spot; nothing but the bald rolling prairie." And, we might add, railroad and town speculation.

Railroad rights-of-way were strictly utilitarian. What one saw out of a train window was usually viewed through an array of telegraph poles and wires. John Kouwenhoven wrote of a train trip

between St. Louis and Chicago on the Wabash Railroad: "Running alongside the track all the way, three tiers of shining wires dip from and rise to the crossbars on the telegraph poles—each of the three crossbars with room for ten bright insulators, some missing, leaving gaps like broken rake teeth." Only the towns interrupted the monotony of farm fields quickly flashing by, and then mainly with views into the back recesses of small-town life: the neglected backyards, the backs of stables and garages, the overflowing trash containers. Then came the lumberyards, the coal yards, and the tanks for oil storage. Understandably, postcard publishers had little interest in picturing most of what train passengers saw. But the depot was invariably pictured.

Just as towns could not thrive without a railroad, so with the coming of automobiles and trucks they could not thrive without at least one improved highway. Vandalia, the state capital before Springfield, marked the terminus of the National Road (also called the Cumberland Road) in the nineteenth century. It was the first highway to be federally subsidized, running from Cumberland, Maryland, through and to the state capitals of the relatively new states of Ohio, Indiana, and Illinois: Columbus, Indianapolis, and Vandalia respectively. It was Thomas Jefferson's secretary of the treasury, Albert Gallatin, a strong advocate of "internal improvements," who guided the authorizing legislation for the highway through Congress. In the early twentieth century, the road became part of one of America's early coast-to-coast named highways: the Old Trails National Highway. Later still, the route was marked as U.S. 40. Gallatin Street, Vandalia's main commercial thoroughfare, was in a state of transition when it was photographed in 1910 for the real photo postcard in FIGURE 152A. Only one automobile is visible in the image (probably the photographer's car), along with several wagons and a dozen or so pedestrians. The street is not yet paved, but new curbs and new street lights have been installed . Power lines parallel the street on both sides. New electric signs hang on many storefronts. In the real photo view in FIGURE 152B, produced some twenty-five years later, automobiles and trucks abound on Gallatin Street. Old buildings remain, of course, but their facades are much altered. Streetlights have been upgraded. One power line is gone.

When Illinois became a state in 1818, its first capital was located at Kaskaskia, the former French town on the Mississippi River. A year later, the legislature removed it to Vandalia, where it remained for two decades. Abraham Lincoln and the rest of the "Long Nine," a group of legislators so named because of their height, succeeded in moving it once again, this time to Springfield. It is said that Lincoln lowered himself out of a second-story window in order to dissolve a quorum and prevent a vote that would have kept the legislature at Vandalia another twenty years. From 1839 to 1933, the old capitol building served as the Fayette County Courthouse.

Pictured in FIGURE 153 is a "Madonna of the Trail" statue in front of the Vandalia state capitol building, one of several such statues erected by the National Old Trails Association (in conjunction with the Daughters of the American Revolution) under the direction of Harry S. Truman, who was the organization's head at the time. In addition to putting up directional signs, the association published maps and guidebooks orienting motorists to the National Road, which was reborn in the years after World War I as an auto route. Farther west it followed a reborn Boone's Trace across Missouri and a reborn Santa Fe Trail westward from Truman's Kansas City into New Mexico and to the Pacific Coast beyond. Named highways, the so-called "blazed trails" of Rand McNally road atlases and maps, preceded the nation's numbered highway system, which was introduced in the 1920s. The route of the National Old Trails Road became U.S. 40 across Illinois.

As the new state capital, Springfield, boomed, Vandalia settled down to being a small farm town and the seat of Fayette County. However, improved highways, like the railroads a half-century before, promised more. Crossing the east-west U.S. 40 at Vandalia was the north-south U.S. 51, earlier dubbed "the Egyptian Trail." Town boosters in Vandalia, like those in many towns and small cities across the state, formed an investment syndicate to build a new hotel, the Hotel Evans (FIGURE 154). The intention was to attract automobile tourists as well as traveling salesmen and other businesspeople, most of whom now arrived by automobile rather than by train. "There is always one leading hotel in or near the central crossroads," Graham Hutton observed of the typical midwestern community, "and the lobby chairs are nearly

FIGURE 152A. Gallatin Street, Vandalia, ca. 1910.

FIGURE 152B. Gallatin Street, Vandalia, ca. 1935.

FIGURE 153. "Madonna of the Trail" statue, Vandalia, ca. 1930.

Hotel
Evans

Vandalia, Ill.

90 Rooms
4 Suites
5 Stories
With
Roof Garden

ON THE "MAIN STREET" OF THE U.S.A. "THE NATIONAL OLD TRAILS ROAD" AT VANDALIA, ILL.   99266

FIGURE 154. Hotel Evans, Vandalia, 1924.

FIGURE 155. Lincoln Highway, Niles Center, ca. 1920.

always occupied. Here meet for lunch, on their respective days, if the town is large enough, the Rotarians, Lions, Elks, Kiwanis, Buffaloes, or other service clubs; banquets are given; and local functions take place. It is one of the very few common meeting-places. On the mezzanine or the second floor is usually the local Chamber of Commerce, if the town boasts one."

The Lincoln Highway, connecting New York City with San Francisco, was another of the named highways to cross Illinois. Where roads were nonexistent along the surveyed route, as, for example, across parts of Utah and Nevada, the Lincoln Highway Association, funded by member subscriptions and corporate donations, actually built stretches of new road. In promoting "good roads," the association also created "demonstration miles"—hard-surfaced stretches of modern highway that were landscaped and lit at night—

roadways suggestive of what a national system of modern highways might one day be like. The Lincoln Highway bypassed Chicago, passing only through the city's southernmost and westernmost suburbs. At Niles Center, it cut west across the state through DeKalb and Dixon to Fulton, in a stretch that later became U.S. 30 (FIGURE 155). Just as towns in the nineteenth century had competed vigorously for county government, and then had worked hard for railroad connections, so in the twentieth century they competed for improved highways. For a town not to be on a modern highway was to invite certain decline.

Pana was a coal-mining town located some thirty miles north of Vandalia on U.S. 51. It called itself the "Rose City." Smokestacks rose above coal-heated greenhouses within which acres and acres under glass were planted mainly in roses intended primarily for the Chicago market. Pic-

FIGURE 156. Locust Street, Pana, ca. 1940.

tured in **FIGURE 156** is Pana's main business street in the 1940s, with cars standing angle-parked at the curb. Car ownership in small-town America compelled people to rethink life in terms of dollars and cents. Barter and trade had always been important in small-town business practice, but it was much less so once cash was required for the purchase of a car and the oil and gasoline to run it. As cheaply as Henry Ford might sell cars, their purchase still required cold, hard cash. Automobiles also quickened life, putting towns more in motion. The novelist Ferdinand Reyher struck that chord in describing the fictional town of Sevillinois in *I Heard Them Sing*. At the town barbershop, where much of the novel's action took place, things had changed. "The shrine of leisure and tolerance was no more. An automobile horn honked angrily at the corner, and others blared in irritable response. . . . The time one saved in an automobile one took

from better matters. It had bred impatience. A man always had it on his mind. Standing outside, seemingly inert at the curb, but straining to go. The automobile, that was the untouchable God."

Black coal smoke pours from a factory stack in **FIGURE 157**, bringing prosperity to the small Vermilion County town of Hoopeston. Manufacturers were usually attracted to small towns by the promise of low operating costs. Hoopeston's wage rates, even when compared to those of nearby Danville, were very low, based mainly on seasonal farm work. Farm laborers displaced by mechanization, as well as the wives and daughters of farm families, made for dependable employees. There were numerous small glove and garment factories in Illinois where workers were paid by the piece. In southern Illinois, which was more in the economic orbit of St. Louis, there were many small shoe factories, including those of Brown

FIGURE 157. Canning factory, Hoopeston, ca. 1910.

Shoe and International Shoe. At Hoopeston, however, it was not outside capital that had been invested; Hoopeston developed its own industry, and in the process it encouraged a distinctive agricultural specialty. Wealthy landowners built a cannery and then encouraged their farm tenants to grow and harvest sweet corn. One by one, other canneries opened, as well as small plants to fabricate the cans and cardboard boxes needed to ship the corn to market.

Bridgeport was in the southern Illinois oil field, which centered on Lawrenceville, the seat of Lawrence County, where the Indian Refining Company (later absorbed by Texaco, today's Chevron) opened a refinery. Not far to the north was the larger refinery of the Ohio Oil Company (today's Marathon). Illinois may not be thought of today as a petroleum-producing state, but up through the 1920s it was among the nation's leaders. However,

the largest refineries were built outside the largest cities: east of Chicago in Indiana (Standard Oil of Indiana and Sinclair) and across the Mississippi River from St. Louis (Shell), for example. Pipelines snaked across the state, connecting those refineries not only to the Illinois oil fields but also to oil fields in Texas and Oklahoma. In Bridgeport, crude oil was pumped right at the town's center, even in the backyards of residences (**FIGURE 158**).

Most Illinois towns, even if they had a mine or a factory, remained primarily farm-dependent. Across much of Illinois, that meant a growing emphasis on grain handling: at first corn, and then corn and soybeans. It was the grain elevator rather than the mine tipple or factory smokestack that soared symbolically over small-town rooftops, as exemplified by the postcard from Union in **FIGURE 159**. On the flat Illinois prairies, these "cathedrals of the plains" could be seen for great distances,

FIGURE 158. Oil well, Bridgeport, ca. 1910.

FIGURE 159. Grain elevator, Union, ca. 1925.

clearly marking towns as they arrayed along one or another railroad line. As John Kouwenhoven observed from his Chicago-bound train: "Most of the towns you go through are small . . . with streets at right angles to the railroad. . . . Each town has a corrugated sheet-metal grain elevator and a Quonset warehouse or two near the wooden station. . . . And in less than a minute you are out on the prairie again." Surprisingly, postcard publishers offered relatively few views of grain elevators. Perhaps they were too common a fixture of the landscape.

Located in Logan County, the elevator in FIGURE 159 belonged to the Illinois Traction System, an interurban electric railroad. In the 1930s, various Chicago-area interurban lines were combined under the control of Charles T. Yerkes and given access to the Loop over the tracks of his elevated transit system. Beyond the metropolis, Illinois Traction provided connections to St. Louis from Danville, Champaign-Urbana, Decatur, Bloomington-Normal, Peoria, and Springfield. Most of the state's electric railroads were lightly built, and they deteriorated quickly with use. But the rise of the automobile, in diverting riders away from rail travel, diluted profits and thus made it difficult for the interurban companies, even those owned by powerful utility companies, to finance regular maintenance, let alone capital improvements. In 1960, only two of the state's electric railroads remained, the Illinois Terminal Railroad, successor to the railroad pictured here, and the Chicago South Shore and South Bend Railroad, an important Chicago commuter line.

Schools figured prominently on the typical small-town skyline; the school, including its basketball gym, was often the largest building in town. "Two storied, with unshaded windows regularly spaced on all sides," wrote Rose Wilder Lane of the small-town school, "it rose gaunt above an irregular space of trodden earth on which not a spear of grass survived. Its height was increased and seemed unbalanced by the cupola rising from the eaves above the door. A large bell hung there, and when The Principal pulled the rope in the entry below, that bell clanged an iron imperative over the town." Often the school was a town's largest employer. And often it was the town merchants' best customer. The coming of the school bus enabled school consolidation, precipitating not just the closing of one-room country schools but the closing of schools in most of the smallest villages and hamlets as well. The school at Cullom (FIGURE 160A) was located at the edge of town, where the prairie, carved into farm fields, provided a flat horizon.

In addition to its educational functions, the school building served as a community center, especially when football, basketball, and baseball games pitted town against town. The novelty card reproduced in FIGURE 160B celebrates the high school in Chrisman, and especially its sports teams. A small felt pennant is glued to the front. This basic template—the picture of a well-dressed coed—lent itself to universal use; by changing the town or school name, the publisher could sell the same postcard in multiple localities.

In small-town Illinois, intellectual matters tended to take a backseat to the practical and the utilitarian. Perhaps it was the leveling aspect of intensive neighboring. To get ahead in a small town, it was essential to go along with the crowd and the crowd's practical instincts. Only in the cities, many Americans believed, was there sufficient anonymity for individuals to be fully individual. And only in the cities was there sufficient wealth and leisure, it was argued, to cultivate life's finer aspects. Small-town people in the Midwest, historian Lewis Atherton concluded, were "addicted to 'things' rather than ideas." Dominant was the cult of the "immediately useful," which had, he added, several important corollaries: (1) cultural matters

FIGURE 160A. Cullom, 1914.

were best "left to women," (2) artistic and intellectual activities needed to conform with "local standards of morality," and (3) they must justify themselves financially. For adults, it was mainly the town library that provided intellectual reach (**FIGURE 161**). Librarians tended to be women—of upstanding morals, of course—who were also excellent managers, willing to operate within meager budgets.

Many small towns across the nation also sponsored Chautauqua celebrations, named for the Chautauqua Lake Assembly near Jamestown, New York, where lectures, music programs, and other forms of entertainment had become an integral part of summer vacationing. Under the direction of the assembly, lecturers, artists, and others moved from town to town across the United States, bringing to otherwise culturally isolated places what passed as edifying uplift. The Chau-

tauqua circuit was related to the even older lyceum movement, which had brought "culture" to small towns in the winter months, using the auditoriums of lodge halls and "opera houses." Many towns developed parks, complete with large pavilions, in which annual Chautauqua events, usually lasting an entire week in summer, might be celebrated. The postcard view in **FIGURE 162** shows the park and pavilion in Mason County's Havana. Handwritten across the bottom are the words "This is a first rate place & great things going on all the time."

Lumber for houses like the Woodford County home in Metamora pictured in **FIGURE 163** was relatively cheap early in the twentieth century, most of it distributed from Chicago. The labor costs for constructing such a house were relatively modest as well. Thus an enthusiasm for large, and often drafty, multistory houses swept the Midwest late in the nineteenth century, especially across the wealthier north. "Across the front of the house," wrote novelist Rose Wilder Lane, "there was invariably a porch. At least one hickory rocker stayed on it in all weathers; on summer afternoons other chairs would be brought from the house and children sat on the steep porch steps." Such porches figured prominently in small-town childhoods. Poet Dave Etter mused:

> I grew up in a morning-glory town
> under a cathedral of giant elms,
> a carefree banger of screen doors,
> a smug loafer and laugh getter
> on all the gingerbread porches.

Few families in the typical town ever felt the need for a professional architect. Builders' manuals, carpentry guides, and even catalogs sufficed, from which prefabricated houses might be ordered from companies such as Sears and Montgomery Ward. Lewis Atherton wrote: "Owners wanting a measure of individuality were advised to add jig-saw railings and gingerbread decorations. These embellishments supposedly made a plain house 'tasty.'"

Early in the twentieth century, American small towns were considered the best place to raise children. The town, it was said, was a microcosm of the larger world, but one that, despite its small size, was highly personalized, its residents like a big, extended family—an ideal place, in other words, for young people to learn about life. With small populations occupying constricted spaces somewhat isolated from the outside world (at least before the coming of widespread automobile use), small-towners had a lot of interaction. City life, in contrast, was thought to be cold and impersonal, and potentially alienating. More ambitious small-town youths usually moved to cities as adults, although later in life they would muse nostalgically about their small-town roots.

FIGURE 160B. Novelty postcard, Chrisman, 1908.

The affluent middle class formed the backbone of small-town society: the families of merchants, professional people, and successful artisans as well as bankers and factory owners. As business owners, they gave their town its measure of success. But by 1900, small-town economics was already proving problematic. Large city-based corporations had come to enjoy unprecedented economic power, substantially stifling to traditional ways of making and marketing things at

FIGURE 161. The Hammond Library, Geneseo, ca. 1915.

FIGURE 162. Chautauqua Park, Havana, ca. 1905.

FIGURE 163. Residence, Metamora, ca. 1910.

the local level. There may have been no other politician in America who surpassed William Jennings Bryan in the ability to assert small-town values. **FIGURE 164** shows him striding up the front walk of a supporter's house in Lena, where he had come to give a speech. Bryan was born in Salem, in southern Illinois, and launched his law career in Jacksonville, but it was after he had moved on to Lincoln, Nebraska, that he embarked upon a political career that would make him the Democratic Party's nominee in three presidential elections. Bryan became the voice of the discontented: the nation's small farmers, its shopkeepers, and the unemployed and underemployed. He argued for cheaper money through the coinage of silver, and for an end to the gold standard. He opposed the growth of "trusts," whereby single corporations were able to dominate whole industries. In a sense, he opposed the economic forces that were

making big cities such as Chicago even bigger. Bryan's visit to Lena was an event to celebrate. A local photographer had come to record his arrival.

Poet and essayist Carl Van Doren, who grew up in central Illinois, described the mythical small town: "There it lay in the mind's eye, neat, compact, organized, traditional: the white church with tapering spire, the sober schoolhouse, the smithy of the ringing anvil, the corner grocery, the cluster of friendly houses; the venerable parson, the wise physician, the canny squire, the grasping landlord softened or outwitted in the end; the village belle, gossip, atheist, idiot; jovial fathers, gentle mothers, merry children; cool parlors, shining kitchens, spacious barns, lavish gardens, fragrant summer dawns, and comfortable winter evenings." The small town was at base a predictable, safe, good-hearted place. It was this sort of "happy days" thinking that large commer-

FIGURE 164. William Jennings Bryan, Lena, August 22, 1911.

cial postcard publishers embraced when they produced views of small towns—if they did so at all (**FIGURE 165**). It was the sort of positive thinking that snapshots, when converted to postcards for mailing, tended to reinforce.

FIGURE 166 depicts a foursome of small-town friends who had visited a photo studio to have their "likenesses" taken. The photographer quickly obliged, making up prints for them to take along. The personal message on the back of this card is addressed to "Dear Old Maid." It reads: "The bunch was out for a time Sunday and this is what happened." It is signed "Dutch," who was probably of German descent. When young males bonded, they sometimes caused much mischief. But those pictured here seem to be good citizens. Dutch, likely a bachelor, was perhaps beginning to think seriously about the gentler sex. Such postcards offer today a candid view of life as once lived; they

insert the viewer into a past social situation and not just a place.

America's entry into World War I fostered an outpouring of patriotic fervor. Young men from farm and small-town families were especially responsive to the call to arms. Opportunities had become restricted in rural Illinois, and the wider world may have seemed most alluring. In addition, the highly personalized relationships that people from farms and small towns maintained with one another made it more difficult for young men to resist a locality's enthusiasm for enlistment. Small-town Americans organized to sell war bonds, collect scrap metal, and make bandages. For the most part, they supported the federal government's search for spies and other subversives, and they condoned the punishment of pacifists. In many locales, they harassed German Americans. The teaching of German was dropped

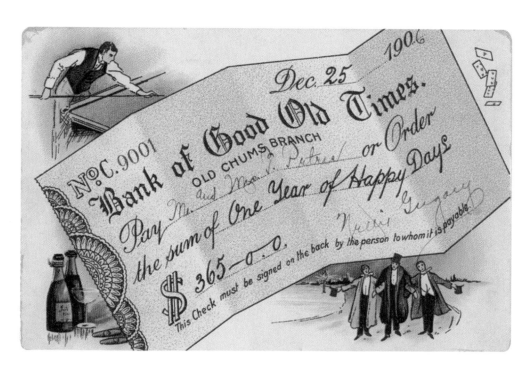

FIGURE 165. Novelty postcard, ca. 1905.

from schools. Ministers in German American areas stopped conducting services in their native language, and many families anglicized their names, the Schmitts becoming the Smiths, for example. Photographers pictured the times—not just producing portraits, especially of those fresh in uniform (FIGURE 167), but also depicting war-related public events, including political rallies, parades, and troop train departures. The carefree nature of small-town life, if ever it was carefree, seemed like another world once a soldier reached the trenches of Europe's front lines.

Postcards with a holiday theme were popular (FIGURE 168), an early version of the folding cards that the greeting-card industry eventually induced most Americans to send in envelopes. Church spires punctuated many a small-town skyline, competing for prominence, in a sense, with grain elevators and water towers. Church

FIGURE 166. Charlie, Baldy, Swede, and Dutch, ca. 1905.

to generation, an important impulse to family rootedness in a place. But where churches had mainly American roots, and especially where the dominant churches had originated west of the Appalachians—Methodists, Baptists, Disciples of Christ, and the other Protestant sects born of frontier evangelism—people tended to be more footloose, more likely to leave a community when seemingly better opportunities presented themselves elsewhere.

In small-town churches, and in country churches as well, theological issues tended not to excite. A new priest or minister quickly learned to avoid doctrine. "He confines his sermons to the things in which the people are interested," observed several University of Illinois sociologists, "their prosperity, sickness and health, the land and its products, the blessings of God. He has learned, too, to chastise the people for their sins and lapses in daily living. They expect the church to comfort them in trouble, to exhort them in their indifference, to point out the sources of their happiness and prosperity."

New technologies affected small towns no less than cities, although usually later, innovation tending to move down rather than up urban hierarchies. With the coming of the automobile, the typical doctor's geographical range was vastly expanded, and even farm families at some distance from a town could count on house calls. By 1915, many Illinois communities had organized telephone companies with central switchboards, often operated by women. Other towns merely waited for a city-based telephone company to string its lines their way. In medical emergencies, doctors could be readily summoned by telephone, as the advertising card in FIGURE 169 suggests. Grocery orders could be easily phoned in as well. In addition, the telephone helped to amplify small-town gossip. Vachel Lindsay observed that gossip was on the rise in the countryside, too; the party-line phone, common to farm families, en-

congregations varied by kind and importance from one locality to the next. Especially in farm communities that were rooted in German and Scandinavian nativity, one or another church congregation—be it Roman Catholic, Lutheran, Mennonite, Apostolic Christian, or another European Protestant sect—provided the social glue that bound locals tightly together. For many such congregants, landownership represented a form of patrimony to be passed from generation

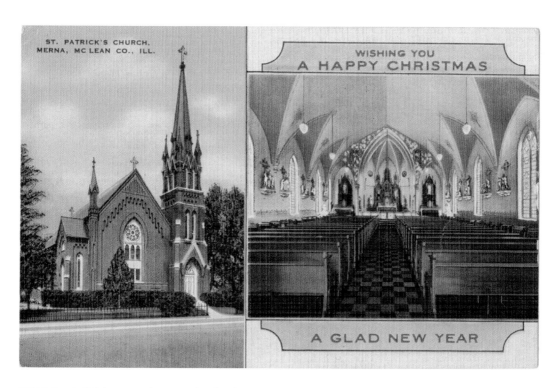

FIGURE 168. Holiday postcard, St. Patrick's Church, Merna, ca. 1930.

FIGURE 169. Advertising postcard for the American Telephone and Telegraph Company, ca. 1925.

FIGURE 170. The First Trust & Savings Bank, Harrisburg, ca. 1930.

abled neighbors to talk to one another all at once. "In the evening everyone takes down the receiver. The conversation goes round the circle, as it used to do at the post-office-store, but the group is larger, and the ladies join in."

Radio was another innovation that helped break down small-town and rural parochialism. In **FIGURE 170**, the transmitter towers of a new radio station crown the roof of Harrisburg's new skyscraper, the tallest building at the time in southern Illinois. People in Harrisburg were obviously

adapting to the forces of modernity. "These forces," wrote Illinois State University sociologists John Kinneman and Richard Browne, "are represented in the circulation of daily papers, free delivery of mail, widespread installation of telephones, construction of arterial highways and the improvement of secondary roads, consolidation of schools, electrification and other modernization of farm houses, reliance upon the cities for radio transmission, and acceptance of hospitalization and generally in a wider adherence to city ways of doing things." Quality-of-life differences between the Chicago metropolis and downstate cities and towns diminished steadily and often quite quickly.

Few technical innovations excited Americans as quickly as radio. When Chicago station KYW went on the air in 1921, there were fewer than 200 radio receivers within listening distance; two months later, there were more than 20,000. At first, listeners downstate tuned in to the big-city stations. But one small Douglas County town proved to be an innovator. WDZ in Tuscola was operated by a grain elevator, broadcasting grain and livestock prices every hour, and filling the between times with music both recorded and live. The duo of Red and Pearl, pictured in **FIGURE 171** with their guitars, entertained in the years just after World War II, sponsored by Wait's Green Mountain Cough Syrup. In the 1940s, television began to further open small-town and rural Illinois to the same national influences that impacted big cities. Looking out of his train window, John Kouwenhoven studied TV antennas: "The height of those antennas measures the strength of the city's pull," he concluded. "As you leave St. Louis they grow taller and taller until in central Illinois they outtop and almost outnumber the trees. As you approach Chicago they grow shorter until, when you reach the suburban landscape of supermarkets, drive-ins, and rows of little square houses with little square lawns, they need be only small, solicitous bundles of branching wire rods attached to the house chimneys."

Postcard publishers tried to portray small towns as up-to-date and future-oriented. That was what small-town customers expected. But some cards were fully backward-looking. They pictured things thought to be "historic," not just old objects roped off or under glass in museums, but whole sections of cities or small towns that, for one reason or another, had not changed much over the years. The building at Old Shawneetown in FIGURE 172 is an obvious relic of the past: it was built in 1839 to house a branch of the United States Bank. Shawneetown, in Saline County, had been an important crossing place on the Ohio River for early Illinois settlers coming overland from Kentucky and Tennessee, as it had also been an important debarkation point for settlers coming down the river by flatboat from as far away as Pennsylvania. Nearby were important salt works. Legend has it that Chicago merchants seeking a loan with which to improve the Chicago River as a harbor were turned down by the bankers in Shawneetown, who told them that Chicago was simply too far away to ever amount to anything. After a devastating flood in 1938, most of the town's houses were subsequently moved to high ground at what is now New Shawneetown; new business buildings were constructed there in the style of 1950s suburban shopping centers.

Galena, in Jo Daviess County, has always been Illinois's best-preserved urban place; many of its buildings have survived from the early decades of the nineteenth century, the town's glory days as a lead-mining center. As the editors of a Depression-era state guide observed, Galena's streets offer "a resume of the nation's architectural experience. Along the terraces of Bench, Prospect, and High Streets, are stately Greek Revival mansions of brick, imposing in size and romantic in setting." The Victorian era, they concluded, "swept over

FIGURE 171. Red and Pearl souvenir postcard, WDZ Radio, Tuscola, ca. 1945.

Galena lightly, and the scourge of gingerbread brackets and scrolls ... is less virulent here." In a postcard view from the 1950s (FIGURE 173), old storefronts edge both sides of a curving main street, a vista that, in addition to its historical significance, is inviting to photography and to postcard representation.

It was from Galena that Ulysses S. Grant left for the Civil War. "The sleepy town of Galena," wrote the editors of *Holiday* magazine, is "known

FIGURE 172. The City National Bank Building, Shawneetown, ca. 1900.

FIGURE 173. Main Street, Galena, ca. 1960.

FIGURE 174. Ulysses S. Grant family home, Galena, ca. 1920.

now as the spot where in April of 1860 a stoop-shouldered, middle-aged little man came to clerk for his younger brothers in a leather-goods store after whisky had ruined an Army career. He had failed as a farmer, real-estate agent and tanyard employee, and was to fail again as clerk. But a year from then he was teaching close-order drill to the Jo Daviess [County] Guards, and five years from then he was to accept the surrender of Robert E. Lee at Appomattox." After the war, the grateful citizens of Galena presented the Grant family with the house pictured in **FIGURE 174**, in which the family had resided for short periods both before and after Grant's presidency. Since 1904, it has been open to the public as a museum. The caption on this postcard reads in part: "The parlor in the General U. S. Grant home has the original horsehair covered walnut furniture.... The vases on the mantel are of Bohemian glass ..., a gift to the Gen-

eral while on his world tour." Americans tended to like their history separated out and presented in museums. The past was not something to be embraced as a part of everyday life. Its picturing offered remembrance, but not necessarily a template for living life day to day or for anticipating the future.

ILLINOIS FARMS

Beyond Illinois's cities and towns lay open country where farms predominated. Many Americans thought that beyond its largest cities, especially Chicago, farming was all the Middle West as a region had to offer. In Illinois, agricultural output varied from one part of the state to another: dairying in the north along with truck gardening near Chicago; raising corn and hogs in the west; and dairying, poultry raising, and peach and apple growing in the far south. But it was the vast grain

FIGURE 175. Farm, McLean County, ca. 1910.

region across the east-central portion of the state that tended to register most with visitors. Driving south out of Chicago on a summer's day, one saw corn and more corn, "waving in the breeze of early morning, shimmering in the heat of noonday sun, in long swells, in quiet planes, from the highway to the horizon." Anchoring each farm was a house with a dooryard garden and perhaps a small orchard nearby, a barn with a night pasture for draft animals, a windmill with a well or washhouse, and various auxiliary buildings, including chicken coops and woodsheds. Fields were fenced, usually with barbed or woven wire, although there were also numerous relic hedgerows planted before cheap wire fencing had become available. "The farmhouses and farm buildings of the Midwest are, to a stranger, uniform, somewhat severe but clean, solid, and handsome," Graham Hutton reported. "All the houses are white, wood-frame,

and either rectangular or L-shaped, with the front porch and entrance in the crook of the L." It was not unusual for proud homeowners to have postcard views made of their houses, which they could share with friends and family. Written on the back of the real-photo postcard in FIGURE 175 is the message: "How do you like our home? Trust you will get out some day. Crops are fine. Will is plowing for the third time."

In another intimate real-photo view, farm folk sit chatting outside a house in Vermilion County (FIGURE 176). In this photograph there is a strong suggestion of what author Lyell Henry called "prosperity, tranquillity, and happiness down on the farm." Were not farmers the "chosen people of God," and was not farming thus the proper foundation for America? Popular thinking early in the twentieth century still saw the nation's farmers as the wellspring from which the American ex-

FIGURE 176. Farmhouse, Vermilion County, August 19, 1916.

perience had been repeatedly revived. Journalist Graham Hutton put it this way: "The severe self-reliance in the farmer's struggle with soil and elements, his geographical isolation from others most of the time, individual responsibility for his acts and decisions, the dependence of his kith and kin and way of life on those acts and decisions, the headship of his little family-community in its isolated acres—all these things make him tend to bring up his children with a sense of the hardness and unpredictability of life." In 1900, there were 250,000 farms in Illinois, with an average size of 124 acres. But more than half of the state's population already resided in urban places.

Illinois farmers might have considered themselves an "elect" people, but they also tended to feel exploited. "Their attitude has always been that of the debtor to his creditor," Hutton asserted. "This colors their attitude to monetary problems,

to industrialism and industrial capitalism, and, if they are tenants, to landlords." During World War I, commodity prices rose, and farm production, aided by steam tractors and threshing machines, increased sharply. But during the postwar recession of the 1920s, prices declined, only to fall steeply with the onset of the Great Depression. The typical farmer was not able to adjust expenses to income. If farmers collectively enlarged their output when demand was stable or falling, the result was overproduction and lower commodity prices. Modern farming increasingly relied on fertilizers, herbicides, field drainage, and, importantly, motorized machinery. All of these things were necessarily purchased in a money economy. Should the farmer abandon modern methods and revert to something like a subsistence existence enhanced as before with local barter and trade, the capital invested in modernization was lost.

FIGURE 177. Threshing, near Homer, ca. 1916.

But then "neither could he close down the farm because his fixed charges, taxes and interest must be met and his livestock must be fed whether farming pays or not."

Illinois farmers conformed to what Hutton calls "a routine and pattern of life ... partly prescribed by Nature, partly by tradition, partly by the compelling force of local uniformity." Before the widespread adoption of modern tractors and harvesters, commercial farmers in Illinois relied heavily on harvesting crews who moved from farm to farm doing contract work. **FIGURE 177** shows a threshing crew contracted to harvest a summer wheat crop in Vermilion County. Pictured in **FIGURE 178** is the end of harvest on a farm near Homer, with the hay for winter animal feed in the process of being stored in the loft of a barn. Huge steam engines and threshing machines required upwards of a dozen men to operate, all of whom had to be fed, a job that invariably fell to the wom-

en on the farm. Wanting to rid themselves of such onerous duty, farm wives, rather than their husbands, often provided the motivation for buying gasoline-powered tractors and combines. By 1950, the majority of Illinois farms had electric power, and thus modern lighting, radios, refrigerators, and vacuum cleaners. Better-off farm women had electric washing machines. Installment buying made it possible. It was not just the main street merchant in the nearby town who prospered accordingly but the large catalog houses such as Chicago's Sears and Roebuck and Montgomery Ward as well.

Few postcard publishers emphasized rural scenes. The market for postcards was largely urban, and urbane; city streets, town squares, and landmark buildings were what sold. By 1900, a move to realism in American literature had produced not only criticism of the small town as parochial and provincial but outright damna-

FIGURE 178. End of harvest, near Homer, ca. 1916.

tion of farms, which were seen as the source of unnecessary privation for most farm families. Authors wrote especially of the arduous life of America's farm women. There was a growing view from the nation's cities that rural people were largely a backward lot. Rural rusticity was not what postcard publishers wanted to picture. Nonetheless, an advertising card such as the one reproduced here in **FIGURE 179** could have limited appeal when properly pitched, especially to America's new suburbanites, and especially to the women who planted and tended the gardens in the nation's new suburbs. Wholesome rural images could be used, and obviously were used, to sell packets of seed to people vicariously living the rural life.

When commercial postcards pictured rural America, it was usually through the lens of social bias. After 1910, urban Americans increasingly encountered farm landscapes as tourists motoring

for pleasure (**FIGURE 180A**). The touristic view was a distanced view that easily lent itself to pictorial stereotype. Postcards needed to speak with quick, hard-hitting visual and verbal messages, and how better to do so than by forcefully reinforcing viewer biases? There was much to discover along rural roads, and postcard publishers were perhaps overly negligent in not better orienting Americans to that fact. "Pull off the highway on a warm, humid night where the road is a mere aisle through a forest of corn," wrote the editors of *Holiday* magazine, "and above the clash and rattle of the shard-like leaves in the constant wind you'll hear a curious brittle popping on every side, a staccato popping like distant firecrackers. That is the corn growing, audibly and enthusiastically." Yet farmers as a group were generally viewed by city people, if not small-towners as well, as provincial and rustic. Farm life was thought to be not only difficult (as it was) but also constricting in

FIGURE 179. Advertising postcard for the H. W. Buckbee Company, Rockford, ca. 1915.

in Illinois, especially on the prairies with their vast horizons. Edgar Lee Masters pondered the apparent endlessness of it all:

> To contemplate the prairies is
> To fathom time, to guess at infinite space,
> To find the Earth-spirit in a dreaming mood.
> In Illinois the prairies are a soul,
> A muse of distance eyeing the solitude.

For John Kouwenhoven, who was confined to a train seat, there was not so much mystery. Modernity had arrived. "The prairie has become, in fact, a technological landscape: subdivided by wire fences, smoothed by tractors, tied to the urban-industrial world by wires, roads, and rails."

Illinois beyond the metropolis was the heartland. For one thing, wrote Donald Culross Peattie, it was fully American in its "unappreciated beauty of plainness." Thus the Illinois countryside was beautiful "as only a great fertile plain can be beautiful." "If I cannot have a range of snowy mountains," he begged, "then give me a great teeming plain." In Illinois you could see "right down to the horizon." "You have 180 degrees of an arc of sky, be it the aching blue of spring . . . or a sky with vast moving clouds . . . in the days of summer thunderheads." And it was measured landscape as well: "relative flatness ruled of by roads and fences in mathematical precision." "White roads struck straight tangents to distant horizons as if taped across the land."

SECTIONAL DIFFERENCES IN ILLINOIS

A network of "hard roads," as most Illinoisans put it in the 1920s, bound the state together—socially, economically, and politically—as never before. Increased automobile use began to break down sectional differences across the state that had been evident from the time of early settlement: Yankees to the north, people with roots in the Middle

both a geographical and a social sense, opening rural Americans up to ridicule. As FIGURE 180B shows, however, this did not stop farm communities from poking fun at themselves.

Isolation was indeed the great resister to city influences. Improve the byways, the "Good Roads" advocates argued, and hasten thereby modernity, if not urbanity (FIGURE 181). No small town need be left behind. However, distances did seem great

FIGURE 180A. Novelty postcard, ca. 1915.

FIGURE 180B. Novelty postcard, ca. 1915.

FIGURE 181. U.S. 54 near Pittsfield, ca. 1925.

Atlantic states in the center, southerners to the south, and various immigrant groups spread across the state. Southern Illinois may have exhibited the most in the way of cultural differences—the "Other Illinois" it has been called in recent decades. Since the early nineteenth century, it has also been referred to as "Egypt" (FIGURE 182). In the 1830s, or so legend has it, a severe winter followed by a summer drought brought widespread crop failure upstate. "But in southern Illinois rain fell and there were good crops, and from the north came people seeking corn and wheat as to Egypt of old," wrote Baker Brownell. Often defined as that part of the state below U.S. 40, "Egypt" featured combined landscapes of "magnolias, southern pine, and northern oak; verdant bottom lands and Ozark plateaus; orchard-covered hills, corn and cotton fields; coal mines, bass lakes, and a magnificent rendezvous for Canadian geese."

Cairo epitomized the "Egypt" idea both by name and by its location where the two great rivers (the Ohio and the Mississippi) met at the top of an extensive delta that stretched south to the Gulf of Mexico. It was laid out on a narrow peninsula just north of the river confluence, a seemingly logical place for a river town. In fact, it was the Illinois Central Railroad, and the role it played in outfitting the Union Army's Civil War campaigns in the Lower Mississippi Valley, that put Cairo on the map. It was the railroad that built the levee, thus providing protection from floods. And it was the railroad bridge, opened after the Civil War when the railroad was being extended south to Memphis and New Orleans, that enabled Cairo to become the quintessential river-crossing town, and something of a small city. It became an important area for lumber milling while the Mississippi Delta was being stripped of its hardwoods.

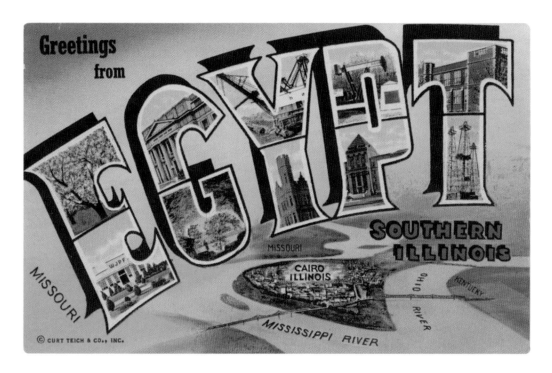

FIGURE 182. Novelty postcard, ca. 1940.

Pictured in FIGURE 183 is the downtown business street along the Ohio River in Cairo. On Saturdays, as described by the Federal Writers' Project, it was "astir with growers of corn, cotton, and apples, who arrive in clay-splattered cars to shop, see a movie, and observe the city sights. At such times Negro boys jig on the levee for the pennies of the passerby, and Negro jug bands play on street corners for pitched coins. The hot-tamale man appears at dusk, pushing his wares in a box fixed on a perambulator chassis." Although steamboats could still be seen berthed along Ohio Street through the 1920s, the river traffic was dominated by barges. Lashed together and pushed by towboats, they were loaded with grain, coal, sand, and other bulk commodities. Cairo's African Americans worked at various low-paying jobs, the men as laborers at lumber mills or cottonseed-processing plants or as roustabouts on the levee, and the women as cooks

in restaurants or domestic servants. Both the economic makeup of southern Illinois small towns and the social stratification within them reflected southern ways. Cairo, after all, was closer to New Orleans than it was to Chicago.

ILLINOIS'S WILDER PLACES

As the state's forests were cut down and its wet prairies and riparian marshlands were drained, natural landscapes and places were obliterated. Only a few relic sites survived unspoiled. Illinoisans in cars still spilled out of the towns and cities in search of nature, but what they found was usually farm scenes that seemed nature-like. Early in the twentieth century, their quest for natural places was part of an anti-urban impulse that helped to underpin the growth of city suburbs with their country club golf courses. But when nature was found, most Americans reduced it to familiar

View of Ohio Levee, looking South from 8th St. Cairo, Ill.

FIGURE 183. Ohio Street, Cairo, ca. 1910.

terms by engaging in activities such as picnicking, an important form of recreation for those on the "open road" (**FIGURE 184**). Both commercial postcards and those derived from snapshots tended to treat nature as a kind of summer place to be filled with picnics. For the amateur photographer, it was clearly a place where friends and relatives smiled and looked at handheld cameras. Wilder places were not always so wild.

Sightseers were attracted to places where nature had largely been spared from human intrusion, especially wilder places that were tinged with the romance of history. Starved Rock was one such locality (**FIGURE 185**). In the 1680s, after the Iroquois Confederacy had attacked the Illinois villages, the French established a fort around which to gather survivors. Some eighty years later, after the great war chief Pontiac was killed near Cahokia, Ojibwa, Ottawa, and Potawatomie warriors

cornered remnants of the Illinois at that place, starving them out and nearly annihilating them. Starved Rock State Park was established in 1912, one of Illinois's earliest. As one authority wrote, the park contained "50 points of interest—canyons, caves, bluffs, and rocks—fancifully or historically named." There was, for example, a "Skeleton Cave," a "Wildcat Canyon," and of course, as depicted here, a "Lover's Leap." River scenery here substantially deviated from what most visitors expected to see in Downstate Illinois. There was strong topographic relief. It was heavily wooded. Everything seemed in sharp contrast to the flat, open prairies just beyond. Obviously, such a place demanded to be pictured in souvenir postcards.

Certainly, Illinois was substantially changed from what Native Americans had known before the arrival of the French. Most of the forests had been cut down, the prairies had been drained and

FIGURE 184. Snapshot, ca. 1915.

Illinois River East from top of Lovers Leap,
State Park View, Starved Rock, Ill.

FIGURE 185. The Illinois River, Starved Rock State Park, ca. 1920.

FIGURE 186. Deer Park, ca. 1910.

plowed under, and even the flow of rivers had been reversed. The "hand of man" had pressed down most forcefully. A conservation ethic, however, was slowly forming. By 1910, Illinois's state park system was rapidly evolving, energized by a public—largely Chicago-based—that was ripe for things "Arcadian." "Arcadia," historian Peter Schmitt explained, was any wild place that lay beyond the city, the focus of "a 'nature movement' led by teachers and preachers, bird-watchers, socialites, scout leaders, city-planners, and inarticulate commuters." Deer Park (**FIGURE 186**), south of North Utica, was originally a private estate, and then a private resort. It later became Matthiessen State Park.

Most visitors to places such as Starved Rock and Deer Park came more to marvel at and wonder about nature than to know and understand it. The back-to-nature movement may have sought spiritual uplift in relatively unspoiled landscapes, but it was a shallow spiritualism at best. People like the group pictured here came to enjoy themselves in a break from town and city routines. Mainly they sought recreation and entertainment. Perhaps the same should be said of postcards—representations that captured the visual outlines of places primarily as pleasurable experience. Postcards did not inform so much as they reminded. They did not convince so much as they predisposed. They did not advocate so much as they suggested. And yet, at base, they remained significant in what they reinforced about landscapes and places.

[ ]

Long before the novelty card in **FIGURE 187** had appeared on a postcard rack, Illinoisans had de-

FIGURE 187. Novelty postcard, ca. 1920.

veloped a kind of split personality regarding who they were as a people. There was urbane Chicago and its suburbs. And, seemingly, there was everywhere else: downstate's small cities, small towns, and farms, somehow all lumped together. Chicago was the big metropolis, Carl Sandburg's "City of Big Shoulders." Chicago was not just the Middle West's primary commercial center but an economic player nationwide as well as globally. Thus was Illinois beyond Chicago readily "othered," not as something fully related, but as something merely lesser, indeed as something much less substantial. And yet Chicago owed its wealth and influence to its hinterland, specifically the resources (material and human) that that hinterland sent its way. Chicago owed its wealth and influence to what it marketed across its hinterland. And the city was part of a political entity

called Illinois. Chicago and Illinois, taken together, stood in mutual symbiosis. But that fact did not keep the stereotyping at bay.

Illinois was a place of small cities, small towns, and farms beyond the Chicago metropolis. As in the big city, little of the original cover of forest and prairie grass survived impulses to turn natural landscapes into civilized places. It was the economic impulse focused on Chicago that drove the whole. Chicago was the central place. But outward from Chicago, oriented first to rivers and canals, then to railroads, and finally to highway and air routes, integrated patterns of economic, social, and political accountability emerged. The Chicago hinterland spread across parts of various midwestern states, but Illinois was foremost. Chicago was in the state of Illinois, which was governed from downstate's Springfield. Shared equally were the badges of political belonging, not the least of which was the legacy left by Abraham Lincoln. Illinois—the Prairie State—claimed Chicago as the Prairie City. Chicago was hesitant to return the favor. But postcard art showed that places beyond the metropolis fully emulated the hinterland relationships. Industrial Chicago was about hogs, cattle, grain, and farm implements. The city's retailing and wholesaling was about marketing all kinds of products, from clothing to lumber, and not just to its own residents but to people beyond. Early-twentieth-century postcard art showed that Illinois's small cities and small towns emulated the lifestyles of the big city by consuming things and services that originated there. Even farm life had begun to take on metropolitan airs. Yet the people of the big city, more sophisticated as some certainly were, still remained dependent on the resources and the markets that lay well beyond. The people of Illinois were in it together.

EPILOGUE

Of what use was the picture postcard? What was the sending and receiving—and the collecting and saving—of postcards all about? How important were the images? A perusal of the short notes that one finds handwritten on vintage postcards is instructive. Reports of travel dominated most of those notations: "Dear Friend. Say, did you know I was away from home and having a good time?" "Say, this is a great place, quite different than Terre Haute." And yes, some senders of postcards were very much interested in what their postcards actually depicted: "Arrived Ok, and I am sightseeing. Will see if this card is showing things right." Postcards were cheaper to send than letters, and with little space for writing, they offered an excuse not to write, or at least not to write much: "Dear Uncle and Aunt. I got your letter, but have been sick. Will write later. Don't worry." A desire to augment a postcard collection was sometimes important: "Dear Unknown Friend. I would like to exchange cards with you."

Whether received in the mail or specifically purchased, picture postcards lent themselves to collecting. Initially displayed in albums to be shown to others or merely stuffed into shoeboxes for safekeeping, the vintage postcards that survive today attest to a once-vigorous culture of visuality, built around strong geographical concerns. Postcards served to legitimize the places they depicted. By picturing places just so, they asserted significance, capable of making even the most ordinary of things into spectacle, or near-spectacle. In addition, the postcard viewer, as spectator, was invited to transcend the moment: to think about what was, but also to think about what had been and what was yet to be. Pictured, of course, were the material things that made up a place, things that were important in and of themselves for some reason but that also signified well beyond themselves. Postcards offered viewers an opportunity to assign meaning: personal importance, certainly, but also, and of greater significance, shared social or cultural meaning. They offered an opportunity to share useful iconography with others.

Fun to look at, convenient to send to others, and easily saved and treasured, postcards proved an excellent surrogate for place experience, a substitute for actually being there. Postcards offered a variety of mechanisms for remembering, for anticipating, or for merely noting aspects of the visual world. That said, however, an additional observation needs to be emphasized here. At least for Chicago and Downstate Illinois, postcard art offered an embrace of the progressive, and, accordingly, a celebration of lifestyles largely urbane. Such, we feel, is the message that underlies vintage Illinois postcard views taken as a whole. Certainly, modernist faith in science, technology, industrialism, and above all urbanism played out in Chicago postcard art. As pictured in postcards, Chicago not only embodied modernity but seemed very much an originator of the modernist project.

Postcards emphasized scenes that spoke reassuringly of an emerging urban future, not just for the Chicago metropolis, but for places well down in the state's urban hierarchy, including the smallest of towns. Even pastoral or natural scenes tended to carry an urban implication: the mechanized farm, the improved highway, na-

ture's potential for recreation. Exposed to view was a fully reassuring America. The fragmented and centripetal nature of life in the United States was largely obscured through the depicting of pacifying, primarily urban unities. The city was a system that was good. Postcard viewers were invited to partake of that system, and to persuade themselves that they were not just part of it but in fact contributors to it. No longer was the city an alienating *Other*. No longer was the city an object that could be viewed only from the outside looking in. Urbanity, as defined in the picture-postcard perfect tense, became a satisfying home base where experiences clustered, to be enjoyed from the perspective of an insider.

Of what use is the vintage postcard to us today? Its quaint charm, of course, is of lasting value. Postcards offer slices of the past caught for an instant by a camera and rendered as a final product through what are now antiquated printing processes. It is difficult to imagine collectors ever losing interest in postcards as visual culture, if only for their value as artifacts. But for scholars and informed general readers, a deeper appreciation of what postcards represent—what they picture and how they picture it—will always provide an intellectual challenge. Vintage postcards appear to be objective representations of past circumstances, but they are also subjective interpretations, the result of socially and culturally conditioned image making.

As landscape views, or as views related to life in specific places, picture postcards enable us to reconstruct the outlines of people's past geographical worlds. They provide us with iconographic checklists with which to assess past geographical knowing. The symbolic power of vintage postcards can be validated today with the benefit of hindsight. But it is sometimes surprising how much of what is pictured in century-old postcards survives today. Even where the things pictured have not been saved, the places often remain functionally the same: similar things, with similar symbolic value, standing in their stead. Life in the past, both in Chicago and in Illinois beyond the metropolis, might be judged as more consistent with life today than most contemporary Americans are wont to admit. Many of the places, or kinds of places, once pictured in postcards—even those places that are very much changed—are still, we think, central to how Americans value and think about their surroundings.

Not that the century-old tourist gaze that launched the postcard industry was any more skewed than the modern or postmodern place interpretations by which we tend to know our contemporary world. Every gaze requires thoughtfulness to understand. What vintage postcards show us, as we have emphasized, hides much. Certainly, visual cliché was at work. Life behind the scenes—where gender, class, racial, and other inequalities thrived—can usually be only implied. Few postcard views offered indisputable proof, for example, of the reactionary forces at work in American society, forces that pitted racial, ethnic, class, and other types of groups against one another. But vintage postcards do invite a sort of "reading between the lines." Taken with other sources of information, they can offer validation for various kinds of understanding—if not by what they show, then by what they do not show.

The humble postcard has lost much of the respect it once enjoyed. Never costing very much, and readily available nearly everywhere, postcards circulated in the hundreds of millions during their earliest decades. But after the glow of faddish popularity had faded, they became something to be taken for granted. As far as the picturing of place was concerned, other media displaced postcards as a means of imagining the world: photography in popular magazines, calendar art, billboard art, glossy tourist brochures, coffee-table

picture books. Then came motion pictures and television with images of landscape and place that actually moved, and for which there were soundtracks. Americans have become more map-literate, especially now that graphics packages are available for home computers and geographical positioning devices for automobile dashboards. These are the visuals that tend to excite today. But let us not forget the picture postcard as visual format. Look around, and you will find that postcards are still for sale. They still arrive in the mail, if only occasionally.

Chicago and the American Middle West may not be as important in the national scheme of things as they once were. Chicago has been displaced by Los Angeles as the nation's second city. No longer is as much steel, or as many farm implements, or as many railroad cars, or as much packaged pork and beef produced in and around Chicago. Many of the traditional icons of Chicago as a place have lost their symbolic power. But others have retained if not increased their power. Chicago remains an important financial center and an important medical center. Its universities continue to thrive. It has become an important research center. It remains a key railroad hub (now very much being revitalized) and a key airport hub as well. It remains an important headquarters city for corporations, but now they are companies that produce such things as aircraft, electronics, and pharmaceuticals.

Downstate cities still make tractors, process soybeans, sell insurance, and, of course, host state government, including the largest of the state's public universities. Illinois still competes to be the nation's principal agricultural state. Everywhere across Illinois, tourism remains important. In Chicago, Grant Park has been remade. In Springfield, a massive new Abraham Lincoln Presidential Library has opened. Much of this activity builds on what Chicagoans and other Illinoisans have long deemed especially significant about their history: significance deeply rooted in the visual images of landscape and place that postcard art helped propagate.

Postcard publishers clearly sought to set Chicago apart as a place. It was the boom town where opportunity thrived on innovation. It was where native-born Americans and new immigrants alike went to prosper. The impersonal metropolis meant freedom to experiment and to change unhindered by the tyrannies that the intimacies of living in small, inwardly focused communities tended to impose. Familiarity in small places bred social conformity, it was said, perpetuating parochialism. That may have been true. Those who sought comfort in established ways were certainly expected to stay hometown people, if not to remain down on the farm. Early in the twentieth century, most Americans accepted that places such as Chicago were truly different. Lesser places did pale in comparison.

Chicago was certainly different in geographical scale. Specialized land use was fostered—enlarged business districts where office, retail, and entertainment functions focused on specific streets, industrial zones anchored by mammoth factories, wholesaling districts anchored by huge warehouses, and the like. Readily evident was the grand and the monumental. Readily evident were things that lesser places could only mimic. For visitors to Chicago and residents alike, postcard art offered a means of identifying with, and thus participating in, the progress implicit in such grand and monumental things. Irrespective of how common one's life might seem, one could always glory in the uncommon, including the spectacular, and in very personal ways.

For most Chicagoans, however, was life in their metropolis all that different from life in Downstate Illinois? When residents of the city went downtown to experience the big-city modernity that postcard art celebrated, were they not really tourists also? Were they not turning aside from the ordinary to celebrate the extraordinary? To become spectators? Like the postcard publishers, most Americans at the time tended not to pay special attention to the commonplace, the ho-hum of everyday life. The everyday built environment could be dismissed largely as amorphous background, except, perhaps, on special days with special events. In Chicago it was the pervasive grid, most streets meeting at right angles in replication of the section-line patterns inscribed across the rural landscapes of Illinois beyond the metropolis. The everyday came to reside in the flats and bungalows that repeated over and over again, neighborhood to neighborhood, across the city. Commonplace were the business districts strung out along the streetcar and mass transit lines where pedestrian traffic concentrated. At base, was not life in these places very much like that lived in Peoria or in Lincoln? Or in Vandalia, for that matter?

By emphasizing the distinctive and the unusual, however, commercial postcard art helped perpetuate the notion that Chicago and Illinois beyond the metropolis were two distinctive social spheres rather than places where common lifestyles were possible. More importantly, commercial postcards tended to negate the ways in which Chicago and its downstate hinterland were, in fact, closely linked, if not socially, then certainly economically and politically. Privately made snapshots, printed on postcard paper and sent to friends and relatives, established lines of commonality. People in Peoria sat in their backyards enjoying the first warm days of spring just as people in Chicago did. Even in Lincoln, people reinforced gentry predilections by decorating their front parlors in the latest styles. People in Vandalia sought to be modern, whether it was through new street lighting downtown or a brand-new hotel. So also did they struggle, just as those in Chicago struggled, with the untoward of life, whether it be social inequality or something less abstract such as juvenile delinquency or racial prejudice.

Hindsight is an interesting thing. What postcard publishers emphasized early in the twentieth century (the grand and the monumental of metropolitan modernism, it might be called) was not what captured an urbanized America's imagination later in the century. What seems to have excited most were the idealized values of the small community, and a preferred iconography of places rooted more in a romanticized small-town pastoralism. In a sense it was the iconography of place that early postcard publishers had not particularly valued, at least the big commercial publishing houses. Chicago, like all American cities large and small, quickly suburbanized. Cities decentralized through mass automobile ownership and government focus on home ownership, an outgrowth of federal taxing and spending policies initiated during the Great Depression as economic pump-priming incentives. Thus was a version of the American small town replicated in the suburbs, not just through a craving for smaller-scale community per se, but also through a craving to live among the "right people"—people generally better-educated, more affluent, and white. Until recent years, when a substantial historic preservation ethic took hold (sustained by new federal, state, and local tax policies and through a reemphasis on mass transit, among other initiatives), center-city Chicago was very much an evacuation zone—an area depopulated through "white flight."

And yet center-city Chicago's resurgence in recent years has also been driven by the city's touristic implications. The traditional iconography of place that postcard publishers emphasized a century ago has survived and is greatly reinforced. Chicago the monumental, Chicago the grand, continues to attract visitors, generating in people's minds a positive "sense of place." Traditional icons of landscape and place invite investors to invest, business people to pursue profit, shoppers to shop, and of course tourists (and also residents) to recreate. Employment opportunities have brought demand for close-in living, which in turn has revitalized old neighborhoods. At Chicago's center, therefore, the favored scenes of traditional postcard art, although much revised and in many instances much raised in visual power, remain not just to be seen but to be experienced. They are scenes that even today's suburbanites can identify with. They are scenes that midwesterners can take pride in, perhaps especially those from Illinois beyond the metropolis. They are scenes that, over the generations, Illinoisans, if not Americans generally, have been conditioned to appreciate, in part through buying, sending, and collecting postcards. Imagined geographies, as remembered landscapes and places, fulfill actual geographies in interesting ways.

Notes

Preface

P. XI, "HOG BUTCHER FOR THE WORLD": Carl Sandburg, "Chicago," in *Chicago Poems* (New York: Henry Holt & Co., 1916), p. 3.

P. XI, "I SHOULD LIKE TO GO TO AMERICA": Chancellor Otto von Bismarck, quoted in Henry Justin Smith, "Chicago," in *America as Americans See It*, edited by Fred J. Ringel (New York: The Literary Guild, 1932), p. 169.

P. XI, "I ADORE CHICAGO": Sarah Bernhardt, quoted in H. C. Chatfield-Taylor, *Chicago* (Boston: Houghton Mifflin, 1917), p. 3.

P. XI, "FEW GRAPHIC NOVELTIES": Neil Harris, "Postcards from the Quads: Small Cards, Big Picture," *University of Chicago Magazine* 84 (June 1992): 28.

P. XII, POSTCARDS AS WINDOWS AND AS MIRRORS: John Szarkowski, quoted in James Guimond, *American Photography and the American Dream* (Chapel Hill: University of North Carolina Press, 1991), p. 17.

P. XII, THE FLÂNEUR: see Walter Benjamin, *Charles Baudelaire: A Lyric Poet in the Era of High Capitalism*, translated by Harry Zohn (London: New Left Bank Books, 1973).

P. XII, "REDUCING IT TO ACCESSIBLE IMAGES": Dana Brand, *The Spectator and the City in Nineteenth-Century American Literature* (Cambridge, UK: Cambridge University Press, 1991), p. 7.

P. XII, "ENVISIONING": Mike Crang, "Picturing Practices: Research through the Tourist Gaze," *Progress in Human Geography* 21, no. 3 (1997): 362.

P. XII, "REGIMES OF VISUAL MEANING": see John Tagg, "The Discontinuous City: Picturing and the Discursive Field," in *Visual Culture: Images and Interpretations*, edited by Norman Bryson, Michael Ann Holly, and Keith Moxey (Hanover, NH: University Press of New England, 1994), p. 83.

P. XIII, "MINDSCAPING": see Eric Gordon, *The Urban Spectator: American Concept Cities from Kodak to Google* (Hanover, NH: Dartmouth College Press/University Press of New England, 2009).

Introduction

P. 2, "HOW DO I HOLD YOU, CITY": Christopher Morley, "Chicago," in *Old Loopy: A Love Letter for Chicago* (Chicago: Old Argus Book Shop, 1937), p. 1.

P. 2, CONSTRUCTIONIST VIEW OF HISTORY: Richard Handler and Eric Gable, *The New History in an Old Museum: Creating the Past at Colonial Williamsburg* (Durham, NC: Duke University Press, 1997), p. 59.

P. 2, CULTURAL ACCOUTERMENTS OF HEIGHTENED CIVILITY: see Igor Marjanović, "Wish You Were Here: Alvin Boyarsky's Chicago Postcards," in *Chicago Architecture: Histories, Revisions, Alternatives*, edited by Charles Waldheim and Katerina Rüedi Ray (Chicago: University of Chicago Press, 2005), pp. 207–25.

P. 2, "BY PLUCKING BUILDINGS OUT OF THEIR IMMEDIATE SURROUNDINGS": Peter B. Hales, *Silver Cities: The Photography of American Urbanization, 1839–1915* (Philadelphia: Temple University Press, 1984), p. 72.

PP. 2–3, THE VALUES UNDERLYING TWENTIETH-CENTURY POSTCARD VIEWS: Alison Isenberg, *Downtown America: A History of the Place and the People Who Made It* (Chicago: University of Chicago Press, 2004), pp. 53–55.

P. 4, CHICAGO DEMOGRAPHICS: Ernest Ludlow Bogart and John Mabry Mathews, *The Modern Commonwealth, 1893–1918* (Springfield: Illinois Centennial

Commission, 1920), pp. 3, 7, 21; Donald F. Tingley, *The Structuring of a State: The History of Illinois, 1899–1928* (Urbana: University of Illinois Press, 1980), p. 25; Federal Writers' Project, *Illinois: A Descriptive and Historical Guide* (Chicago: A. C. McClurg & Co., 1939), p. 41; Andrew R. L. Cayton and Peter S. Onuf, *The Midwest and the Nation: Rethinking the History of an American Region* (Bloomington: Indiana University Press, 1990), p. 38.

P. 4, ILLINOIS CORN PRODUCTION: Federal Writers' Project, *Illinois*, p. 73.

P. 4, CRUDE OIL PRODUCTION: Tingley, *Structuring of a State*, p. 64.

P. 5, FRENCH COLONIAL SETTLEMENT: see Carl J. Ekberg, *French Roots in the Illinois Country: The Mississippi Frontier in Colonial Times* (Urbana: University of Illinois Press, 1998).

P. 6, ILLINOIS'S MARKET ECONOMY: see Michael P. Conzen, "The Historical and Geographical Development of the Illinois and Michigan Canal National Heritage Corridor," in *The Illinois and Michigan Canal National Heritage Corridor: A Guide to Its History and Sources*, edited by Michael P. Conzen and Kay J. Carr (DeKalb: Northern Illinois University Press, 1988), pp. 3–25; William Cronon, *Nature's Metropolis: Chicago and the Great West* (New York: W. W. Norton, 1992).

P. 6, THE ILLINOIS CENTRAL RAILROAD: see James E. Davis, *Frontier Illinois* (Bloomington: Indiana University Press, 1998).

PP. 8–9, CHICAGO AS A FINANCIAL CENTER: Conzen, "Historical and Geographical Development of the Illinois and Michigan Canal National Heritage Corridor," p. 96; F. Cyril James, *The Growth of Chicago Banks* (1938; reprint, New York: Harper & Row, 1969), p. 444.

P. 9, CHICAGO VS. ST. LOUIS: Wyant Winton Belcher, *The Economic Rivalry between St. Louis and Chicago, 1850–1880* (1947; reprint, New York: AMS Press, 1968), pp. 114–17; J. Christopher Schnell, "Chicago versus St. Louis: A Reassessment of the Great Rivalry," *Missouri Historical Review* 71, no. 3 (1977): 265.

P. 9, VON THÜNEN'S CENTRAL PLACE THEORY: John C. Hudson, *Plains Country Towns* (Minneapolis: University of Minnesota Press, 1985), p. 15.

P. 11, BALLOON FRAMING: Carl W. Condit, *American Building: Materials and Techniques from the First Colonial Settlements to the Present* (Chicago: University of Chicago Press, 1968), p. 43.

PP. 11–12, BIRTH OF THE MODERN SKYSCRAPER: see John Zukowsky, *Chicago Architecture, 1872–1922: Birth of a Metropolis* (Munich: Prestel-Verlag, 1987); Daniel Bluestone, *Constructing Chicago* (New Haven: Yale University Press, 1991).

P. 12, HORSE-DRAWN OMNIBUS LINES: Harold M. Mayer and Richard C. Wade, *Chicago: Growth of a Metropolis* (Chicago: University of Chicago Press, 1969), p. 68.

P. 12, CHICAGO BOOSTERS: see James Gilbert, *Perfect Cities: Chicago's Utopias of 1893* (Chicago: University of Chicago Press, 1991).

PP. 12–13, THE WORLD'S COLUMBIAN EXPOSITION OF 1893: see Reid Badger, *The Great American Fair: The World's Columbian Exposition and American Culture* (Chicago: Nelson Hall, 1979).

P. 13, "MAKE NO LITTLE PLANS": Thomas S. Hines, *Burnham of Chicago: Architect and Planner* (New York: Oxford University Press, 1974), p. xvii.

P. 14, THE *PLAN OF CHICAGO*: see Daniel H. Burnham and Edward H. Bennett, architects, *Plan of Chicago*, edited by Charles Moore (Chicago: The Commercial Club, 1909).

P. 14, FRANK LLOYD WRIGHT: see H. Allen Brooks, *The Prairie School: Frank Lloyd Wright and His Midwestern Contemporaries* (Toronto: University of Toronto Press, 1972).

P. 14, JENS JENSEN: Robert E. Grese, *Jens Jensen: Maker of Natural Parks and Gardens* (Baltimore: Johns Hopkins University Press, 1992), pp. 42–51.

P. 14, MIGRATION STATISTICS: see Douglas K. Meyer, *Making the Heartland Quilt: A Geographical History of Settlement and Migration in Early-Nineteenth-Century Illinois* (Carbondale: Southern Illinois University Press, 2000).

PP. 14–15, IMMIGRANTS IN CHICAGO: Rudolf A. Hofmeister, *The Germans of Chicago* (Champaign, IL: Stipes, 1976), p. 16; Donald L. Miller, *City of the Century: The Epic of Chicago and the Making of America* (New York: Simon and Schuster, 1997), p. 442; Irving Cutler, "The Jews of Chicago: From Shtetl to Suburb," in *Ethnic Chicago: A Multicultural Portrait*, edited by Melvin G. Holli and Peter d'A. Jones (Grand Rapids, MI: William B. Eerdmans), pp. 69–108.

P. 15, CHICAGO'S BLACK POPULATION: see St. Clair Drake and Horace R. Cayton, *Black Metropolis: A Study of Negro Life in a Northern City* (New York: Harcourt, Brace & Co., 1945); Allan H. Spear, *Black Chicago: The*

Making of a Negro Ghetto, 1890–1920 (Chicago: University of Chicago Press, 1967).

P. 15, THE LEVEE: Perry R. Duis, *The Saloon: Public Drinking in Chicago and Boston, 1880–1920* (Urbana: University of Illinois Press, 1983), pp. 238–40; Duis, *Challenging Chicago: Coping with Everyday Life, 1837–1920* (Urbana: University of Illinois Press, 1998), p. 228.

PP. 15–16, ILLINOIS POPULATION STATISTICS: John Clayton, comp., *The Illinois Fact Book and Historical Almanac, 1673–1968* (Carbondale: Southern Illinois University Press, 1970), p. 42; Robert P. Howard, *Illinois: A History of the Prairie State* (Grand Rapids, MI: W. B. Eerdmans, 1972), p. 567; U.S. Bureau of the Census, *Census of Population* (Washington, DC: U.S. Bureau of the Census, 1960), pp. 14–15.

PP. 16–17, POSTCARD HISTORY: Frank Staff, *The Picture Postcard and Its Origins* (New York: Frederick A. Praeger, 1966), p. 45; Richard Carline, *Pictures in the Post: The Story of the Picture Postcard and Its Place in the History of Popular Art*, new and rev. ed. (London: Gordon Fraser, 1971), pp. 37, 40.

P. 17, THE "PHOTOCHROME" PROCESS: John A. Jakle, *Postcards of the Night: Views of American Cities* (Santa Fe: Museum of New Mexico Press, 2003), p. 24.

P. 17, RAPHAEL TUCK: Staff, *Picture Postcard and Its Origins*, p. 60.

P. 18, BOOKSTORES CONVERTED TO POSTCARD SALES: Miller, *City of the Century*, p. 14.

P. 18, CHICAGO POSTCARD DISTRIBUTERS AND MANUFACTURERS: authors' compilation, based on Reuben H. Donnelley, *The Lakeside Annual Directory of the City of Chicago* (Chicago: Directory Co., 1900–17), and *Chicago: The Great Central Market* (Chicago: Chicago Association of Commerce, 1923, 1928–29).

P. 18, VICTOR O. HAMMON: see Bonnie G. Wilson, *Minnesota in the Mail: A Postcard History* (St. Paul: MHS Press, 2004), p. 128; *Souvenir of Chicago in Colors* (Chicago: V. O. Hammon, 1910); Orville C. Walden, "Reminiscences of an Old Timer," *Post Card Enthusiast* 4 (July 1950): 25.

P. 18, CURT TEICH & CO.: Mark Werther and Lorenzo Mott, *Linen Postcards: Images of the American Dream* (Wayne, PA: Sentinel Publishing Co., 2002), p. 12; Susan Brown Nicholson, "Noted Postcard Archives, Midwestern States," in *Postcard Collector Annual* (Dubuque, IA: Antique Trader Publications, 1997), p. 24.

P. 19, POSTCARD-SIZED PHOTO PAPERS: Jakle, *Postcards of the Night*, p. 26.

Part One. Chicago and Its Suburbs:
The Metropolis

PP. 23–24, GROWTH OF CHICAGO: Philip M. Hauser and Evelyn M. Kitagawa, *Local Community Fact Book for Chicago, 1950* (Chicago: Chicago Community Inventory, University of Chicago, 1953), p. 2.

P. 24, "HERE, MIDMOST IN THE LAND": Frank Norris, *The Pit: A Story of Chicago* (Garden City, NY: Doubleday, Page & Co., 1903), p. 62.

P. 24, "CALL CHICAGO MIGHTY": Julian Street, *Abroad at Home: American Ramblings, Observations, and Adventures of Julian Street; with Pictorial Sidelights* (New York: Century, 1916), p. 139.

PP. 24–25, VISUAL "TABLEAUS": M. Christine Boyer, *The City of Collective Memory: Its Historical Imagery and Architectural Entertainments* (Cambridge, MA: MIT Press, 1994), p. 2.

P. 25, "IF YOU LOOK AT CHICAGO FROM THE AIR": John Ashenhurst and Ruth L. Ashenhurst, *All about Chicago* (Boston: Houghton, Mifflin, 1933), p. 39.

P. 25, "THE CITY HAS A SURPRISING BEAUTY": Graham Hutton, *Midwest at Noon* (Chicago: University of Chicago Press, 1946), p. 149.

P. 27, "THE BELL IN THE CLOCK OF THE BOSTON STORE": Marion Louise Wineman, *Chicago Songs* (Chicago: Will Ransom, 1925), p. 5.

PP. 27–28, "OF COURSE WE VISITED MARSHALL FIELD'S"; "THROUGH GREAT ROOMS FULL OF TRUNKS": Street, *Abroad at Home*, pp. 150, 151.

P. 29, CHICAGO'S FREIGHT TUNNELS: Rand McNally & Co., *Rand McNally Guide to Chicago and Environs* (Chicago: Rand McNally, 1924), p. 162.

PP. 29–30, "WITH YOUR EYES PEPPERED WITH DUST": William Archer, *America To-Day: Observations and Reflections* (New York: Charles Scribner's Sons, 1899), p. 106.

P. 32, "ONLY A BLOCK BEHIND THE BRIGHT FACADE": Morley, *Old Loopy*, p. 20.

PP. 33–34, "LA SALLE STREET SWARMED"; "AT THE ILLINOIS TRUST": Norris, *The Pit*, pp. 78, 79.

P. 34, "BANK BUILDINGS OF THE CITY": Robert Shackleton, *The Book of Chicago* (Philadelphia: Penn Publishing Co., 1920), p. 74.

PP. 34–35, "THE HEAVY ENGINES, RED HOT": Ashenhurst and Ashenhurst, *All about Chicago*, p. 57.

P. 35, "ONE IS STRUCK WITH SOMETHING AKIN TO AWE": "A Triumphant March," Chicago *Inter-Ocean*, April 28, 1885, p. 10.

P. 35, "NOT A SUNKEN AMPHITHEATER SORT OF PLACE": Shackleton, *Book of Chicago*, p. 77.

P. 36, "A GREAT WHIRLPOOL": Norris, *The Pit*, p. 89.

P. 36, "GEOMETRY GONE MAD": Henry Justin Smith, *Chicago: A Portrait* (New York: Century, 1931), p. 46.

P. 36, "UNLIKE OTHER CITIES": Shackleton, *Book of Chicago*, p. 77.

P. 37, "WITHOUT PICTURESQUE APPEARANCE"; "THAT THEY ARE AN AID IN LOADING TRUCKS"; "WHEREVER YOU LOOK": ibid., pp. 78, 82.

P. 38, "BLAME NOT THE ARCHITECTS": Chatfield-Taylor, *Chicago*, p. 31.

P. 41, "THE ENTRANCE-WAY OPENED": Shackleton, *Book of Chicago*, p. 72.

P. 41, BURNHAM-DESIGNED BUILDINGS: Kristen Schaffer, *Daniel H. Burnham: Visionary Architect and Planner*, edited by Scott J. Tilden (New York: Rizzoli, 2003), p. 25.

P. 42, "ON ONE SIDE TOWERING SKYSCRAPERS": *Chicago: The Vacation City* (Chicago: Passenger Department, Illinois Central Railroad, 1930), p. 1.

P. 42, "A COMMON TO REMAIN FOREVER OPEN": see Lois Wille, *Forever Open, Clear, and Free: The Struggle for Chicago's Lakefront*, 2nd ed. (Chicago: University of Chicago Press, 1991), p. 23.

P. 43, "TRAINS . . . CONTINUE TO PUFF": Street, *Abroad at Home*, p. 192.

P. 44, "THERE IS NO OTHER URBAN SKY-LINE QUITE LIKE IT": Smith, *Chicago*, p. 13.

P. 44, "ROSE INTO THE AIR LIKE AN ALLIGATOR'S JAWS": Lloyd Lewis and Henry Justin Smith, *Chicago: The History of Its Reputation* (New York: Harcourt, Brace and Co., 1929), p. 402.

PP. 45–46, "GO TO THE REMARKABLE OBSERVATORY": Hutton, *Midwest at Noon*, p. 150.

P. 47, MARINA CITY: Pauline A. Saliga, *The Sky's the Limit: A Century of Chicago Skyscrapers* (New York: Rizzoli, 1990), p. 190.

PP. 47–48, WRIGLEY BUILDING TILES: Alice Sinkevitch, ed., *AIA Guide to Chicago* (New York: Harcourt, Brace, 1993), p. 100.

P. 48, "AT AN ALTITUDE OF 45,000 FEET": Federal Writers' Project, *Illinois*, p. 242.

P. 49, "THE MOST MONSTROUS OF ALL THE HOTELS": Simone de Beauvoir, *America Day by Day*, translated by Carol Cosman (Berkeley: University of California Press, 2000), p. 95.

P. 49, "THIS IS ONE OF THE FINEST THEATERS IN THE WORLD": Rand McNally & Co., *Bird's-Eye Views and Guide to Chicago: Indispensable to Every Visitor, Containing Innumerable Details of Business and Residence Localities* (Chicago: Rand McNally & Co., 1896), p. 78.

PP. 51–52, "YOU ENTER ANOTHER HOTEL": Shackleton, *Book of Chicago*, p. 81.

P. 52, "CHICAGO IS THE MEETING PLACE OF THE WORLD": *Rand McNally Guide to Chicago and Environs*, p. 150.

P. 52, "AT NIGHT, HIDDEN LIGHTS": Federal Writers' Project, *Illinois*, p. 231.

P. 53, "ASTOUNDINGLY SPLENDID"; "TO THE RIGHT WAS BLACKNESS": Ilya Ilf and Eugene Petrov, *Little Golden America: Two Famous Soviet Humorists Survey These United States*, translated by Charles Malamuth (London: George Routledge & Sons, 1936), p. 107.

P. 53, "A GREAT FLIGHT OF STEPS"; "THE FIRST FLOOR HAS SEVEN HALLS": Harry Hansen, *Illinois: A Descriptive and Historical Guide*, new rev. ed. (New York: Hastings House, 1974), pp. 225, 226.

P. 54, "REGION OF DILAPIDATED BUILDINGS"; "I SELDOM CROSS THE RUSH STREET BRIDGE AFOOT": Chatfield-Taylor, *Chicago*, pp. 5, 11.

P. 55, 1923 LUMBER STATISTICS: *Rand McNally Guide to Chicago and Environs*, p. 155.

P. 55, "WATER CARRYING TRADE": *A Guide to the City of Chicago* (Chicago: Chicago Association of Commerce, 1909), p. 222.

P. 55, "THE RECEIPTS BY WATER"; "ONE OF THE MOST INCONVENIENT AND RESTRICTED HARBORS": George W. Engelhardt, *Chicago: The Book of Its Board of Trade and Other Public Bodies* (Chicago: Chicago Board of Trade, 1900), p. 78.

P. 56, "SUNDAY NIGHT AND THE PARK POLICEMEN TELL EACH OTHER": Carl Sandburg, "Picnic Boat," in *Chicago Poems*, p. 19.

P. 56, THE *EASTLAND* DISASTER: Gerard R. Wolfe, *Chicago in and around the Loop: Walking Tours of Architecture and History* (New York: McGraw-Hill, 2003), p. 159.

P. 56, THE 1871 FIRE: ibid., p. 29.

P. 57, "A NARROW RIBAND OF INKY CURRENT": Engelhardt, *Chicago*, p. 80.

P. 59, "BELOW IS A SUBTERRANEAN PASSAGE": Ashenhurst and Ashenhurst, *All about Chicago*, p. 93.

P. 59, "IT CARRIES AWAY THE SEWAGE": Shackleton, *Book of Chicago*, p. 185.

P. 61, "MAGNIFICENT PINEAPPLES, FOURTEEN DAYS FROM HONOLULU": George E. Plumbe, *Chicago: The Great Industrial and Commercial Center of the Mississippi Valley* (Chicago: Chicago Association of Commerce, 1912), p. 125.

P. 61, "A JAM OF DELIVERY WAGONS AND MARKET CARTS": Norris, *The Pit*, p. 61.

P. 62, "BACKED UP TO [THE SIDEWALKS THERE] ARE TEAMS": Plumbe, *Chicago*, p. 125.

P. 65, THE UNION STOCK YARD; "CATTLEMEN FROM THE PLAINS": *Guide to the City of Chicago*, pp. 160, 161.

P. 65, UNION STOCK YARDS PACKING PLANTS: *Chicago: The Vacation City*, p. 33.

P. 66, "WITH VARYING DEGREES OF SHOCK": Smith, *Chicago*, p. 132.

P. 66, "THE PROGRESS OF THE PIG IS SWIFT": Street, *Abroad at Home*, p. 169.

P. 66, "TO WATCH AN ANIMAL FROM THE PEN TO THE TIN": W. L. George, *Hail Columbia! Random Impressions of a Conservative English Radical* (New York: Harper & Brothers, 1921), pp. 47–48.

P. 67, "PLAYER WITH RAILROADS": Carl Sandburg, "Chicago."

PP. 67–68, "DOWN BELOW THERE, RECTILINEAR": Norris, *The Pit*, p. 61.

P. 68, "IN THE TERMINAL STATIONS OF THE CITY": Edward Hungerford, *The Personality of American Cities* (New York: McBride, Nast & Co., 1913), p. 200.

PP. 69–70, "I WAS WONDERING WHAT CHICAGO WOULD LOOK LIKE": Edgar Lee Masters, *Across Spoon River: An Autobiography* (New York: Farrar & Rinehart, 1936), p. 139.

PP. 70–71, MAINLINE RAILROAD RIGHT-OF-WAY AND BRANCH LINE: *A Guide to the City of Chicago*, p. 221.

P. 71, TRAIN ARRIVALS AND DEPARTURES: Lowe, *Chicago Interiors*, p. 22.

P. 73, "THE STEEL MILLS ARE NOT ORDINARILY OPEN TO VISITORS": Ashenhurst and Ashenhurst, *All about Chicago*, p. 170.

P. 73, "THE CLANNISHNESS OF ORTHODOX JEWS FROM RUSSIA": Edith Abbott, *The Tenements of Chicago, 1908–1935* (Chicago: University of Chicago Press, 1936), p. 88.

P. 75, "A BLEAK AREA OF SEGREGATION": Harvey Warren Zorbaugh, *Gold Coast and Slum: A Sociological Study of Chicago's Near North Side* (Chicago: University of Chicago Press, 1929), p. 9.

P. 75, "THE WEST SIDE HAS ITS SO-CALLED GHETTO": Shackleton, *Book of Chicago*, p. 283.

P. 75, "ALONG THE SIDEWALKS WERE MASSES OF MERCHANDISE": Smith, *Chicago*, p. 158.

P. 76, "FOR DEPTH OF SHADOW IN CHICAGO LOW LIFE": Robert Woods et al., *The Poor in Great Cities: Their Problems and What Is Doing to Solve Them* (New York: Charles Scribner's Sons, 1895), p. 198.

P. 76, "I WAS . . . DEEPLY IMPRESSED BY THE ARRANGEMENTS OF HULL HOUSE": Monsignor Count Vay de Vaya and Luskod, *The Inner Life of the United States* (New York: Dutton, 1908), p. 178.

PP. 77–78, "THOUSANDS UPON THOUSANDS OF NEW, SHABBY, SQUARE WOODEN BOXES": Mary Borden, "Chicago Revisited," *Harper's* 162 (April 1931): 491.

P. 78, "THE VISITOR GENERALLY SEES ONLY THE LOOP": Hutton, *Midwest at Noon*, p. 145.

P. 78, "CHICAGO HAS SUCH ODDITIES": Shackleton, *Book of Chicago*, p. 96.

P. 80, "NORTH AVENUE IS STILL A NORTHERN EUROPEAN THOROUGHFARE": Zorbaugh, *Gold Coast and Slum*, p. 149.

P. 80, "QUICKLY AND EASILY FOLLOW AND ADOPT EVERY AMERICANISM": Julian Ralph, *Our Great West: A Study of the Present Conditions and Future Possibilities of the New Commonwealths and Capitals of the United States* (New York: Harper & Brothers, 1893), p. 18.

PP. 81–82, "THE PEDESTRIANS ARE OF ALL SHADES OF DARKNESS": Smith, *Chicago*, p. 79.

P. 82, "THOUGH CLOSELY HEDGED IN ON THREE SIDES": *Guide to the City of Chicago*, p. 115.

P. 84, "IT WAS A SPECTACLE NEVER TO BE FORGOTTEN": Masters, *Across Spoon River*, p. 209.

P. 84, "THIS GROUP OF BUILDINGS"; "HERE THE INSANE ARE KEPT AWAITING": Rand McNally & Co., *Bird's-Eye Views and Guide to Chicago*, p. 216.

P. 85, "THE HOSPITAL CARES FOR ABOUT 1,100 PATIENTS DAILY": *Guide to the City of Chicago*, p. 197.

PP. 85–86, "YOU HEARD SUCH WONDERFUL THINGS ABOUT [IT]": Edna Ferber, *So Big* (New York: Grosset and Dunlap, 1924), p. 225.

P. 86, "WITH CORBELS AND CROCKETS AND PINNACLES": Shackleton, *Book of Chicago*, p. 249.

p. 88, "on pleasant summer days [chicagoans] go bathing": Hungerford, *The Personality of American Cities*, p. 209.

p. 88, the 1919 race riot: see William M. Tuttle, Jr., *Race Riot: Chicago in the Red Summer of 1919* (New York: Atheneum, 1970).

pp. 88–89, "at the lakeward end is a gigantic auditorium": *Chicago: The Vacation City*, p. 4.

p. 90, "it was a chicago convention that set him on his way": Shackleton, *Book of Chicago*, p. 340.

p. 90, "white city is a noted amusement park": *Chicago: The Vacation City*, p. 4.

p. 92, "these huge steel skeleton towers"; "within this short period man has learned to fly": Ashenhurst and Ashenhurst, *All about Chicago*, pp. 27, 21.

pp. 93–95, "old prairie avenue is a street of ghosts": Smith, *Chicago*, p. 246.

p. 95, "the right place to live": ibid., p. 247.

p. 95, "the real leaders of chicago society": Shackleton, *Book of Chicago*, pp. 202–3.

p. 96, "what other city has begun so nobly"; "chicago is a city of detached houses": Regan Printing House, *Story of Chicago in Connection with the Printing Business* (Chicago: Regan Printing House, 1912), pp. 56, 57.

pp. 96–97, "they were on a street which seemed to run on forever": Upton Sinclair, *The Jungle* (New York: Doubleday, Page & Co., 1906), p. 24.

p. 98, "it is the rule rather than the exception": Walter B. Pitkin, "The American: How He Lives," in Ringel, *America as Americans See It*, p. 201.

p. 98, "deeply recessed center and projecting wings": Shackleton, *Book of Chicago*, p. 331.

pp. 98–100, "people nowadays want a stylish home": Robert Herrick, *The Common Lot* (New York: Macmillan, 1904), p. 154.

p. 101, "in the building there are 25 miles of electric conduit": *Rand McNally Guide to Chicago and Environs*, p. 143.

p. 102, "the town because of its size": *Guide to the City of Chicago*, p. 233.

p. 103, "a beautiful city, ideal": Marian A. White, *Second Book of the North Shore: Homes, Gardens, Landscapes, Highways and Byways, Past and Present* (Chicago: J. Harrison White, 1911), p. 143.

p. 103, "northwestern university is making a distinct contribution": Walter Dill Scott, "North-western University as a Metropolitan Institution," in Rush C. Butler, Jr., comp., *Chicago: The World's Youngest Great City* (Chicago: American Publishers Corp., 1929), p. 92.

p. 105, "if the beauty, majesty and grandeur of this city strike with wonder": Regan Printing House, *Story of Chicago*, p. 73.

p. 105, "in our book evanston was put down as pious": Arthur Meeker, *Chicago, with Love: A Polite and Personal History* (New York: Alfred A. Knopf, 1955), p. 822.

pp. 105–6, "too far from the loop": Ashenhurst and Ashenhurst, *All about Chicago*, p. 145.

p. 106, "each evening at lake forest": James Morris, *As I Saw the U.S.A.* (New York: Pantheon Books, 1956), p. 213.

p. 110, "all structures are of the most classic type": White, *Second Book of the North Shore*, p. 169.

p. 110, illinoisans in the armed services: Hansen, *Illinois*, p. 40.

p. 111, midway airport passenger numbers: ibid., p. 55.

p. 111, "the most impressive first sight of the midwest": Hutton, *Midwest at Noon*, p. 140.

p. 113, "mighty, monstrous, multifarious": Street, *Abroad at Home*, p. 139.

Part Two. Illinois beyond the Metropolis

p. 116, "it's the u.s.a. in a capsule": Clyde Brion Davis, "Illinois," in *American Panorama: East of the Mississippi*, edited by Holiday (Garden City, NY: Doubleday, 1960), p. 187.

p. 116, "it is the heartland": Donald Culross Peattie, "The Best State of the Fifty," *New York Times Magazine*, April 26, 1959, p. SM14.

p. 116, illinois "is core american": David M. Steele, *Vacation Journeys East and West: Descriptive and Discursive Stories of American Summer Resorts* (New York: G. P. Putnam's Sons, 1918), p. 189.

p. 116, "back of chicago the open fields": Sherwood Anderson, "Evening Song," in *Mid-American Chants* (New York: John Lane, 1918), p. 81.

pp. 116–17, chicago river fishery: Hansen, *Illinois*, p. 521.

p. 117, "he was born in kentucky": Henry Horner, "Man of Illinois," in Federal Writers' Project, *Illinois*, p. 46.

PP. 117–18, "NATURALLY, SPRINGFIELD IS SATURATED WITH MEMORY OF LINCOLN": Edgar Lee Masters, *The Sangamon* (New York: Farrar & Rinehart, 1942), p. 213.

P. 118, "TO THIS PLACE AND THE KINDNESS OF THESE PEOPLE I OWE EVERYTHING": Abraham Lincoln, quoted in Karl B. Lohmann, *Cities and Towns of Illinois: A Handbook of Community Facts* (Urbana: University of Illinois Press, 1951), p. 31.

P. 118, "IT IS PORTENTOUS, AND A THING OF STATE": Vachel Lindsay, "Abraham Lincoln Walks at Midnight," in *Collected Poems*, rev. and illustrated ed. (New York: Macmillan, 1925), p. 53.

P. 118, "IN REVERENT DEVOTION": Albert A. Woldman, *Lawyer Lincoln* (Boston: Houghton Mifflin, 1936), p. 1.

P. 119, "THERE IS NONE OF THAT AURA OF DRY ANTIQUITY": Holiday, *American Panorama*, p. 196.

P. 120, "THE EVENT IS ATTENDED BY FARMERS": Masters, *Sangamon*, p. 229.

PP. 120–21, "FROM THE BLUFFS RESIDENTIAL PEORIA COMMANDS A VIEW": Federal Writers' Project, *Illinois*, p. 357.

PP. 121–22, "A DEFINITE IF UNDEFINABLE FLAVOR": Hutton, *Midwest at Noon*, p. 138.

P. 126, "SCATTERED HERE AND THERE"; "ITS KNITTING MILLS"; "FAMED FOR ITS BEAUTIFUL STREETS": Rockford Chamber of Commerce, *Rockford 1912* ([Rockford, Ill.]: Rockford Morning Star, [1912]), pp. 25, 27, 2.

P. 128, "WHEN HE HAD HOISTED THE BUNDLE TO A SHOULDER": Harold Sinclair, *Years of Illusion* (Garden City, NY: Doubleday, Doran & Co., 1941), p. 11.

P. 129, "IT REQUIRES ONLY A REGISTRATION FEE OF THIRTY DOLLARS": Federal Writers' Project, *Illinois*, p. 167.

PP. 130–31, "ALTHOUGH NOT AN INDUSTRIAL TOWN": ibid., p. 179.

PP. 131–32, "SEARCH FOR THE AVERAGE FARMER"; "TO A VISITOR THERE IS SOMETHING OUTLANDISH": Ann Carnahan, "Illinois," in *The United States*, edited by Doré Ogrizek (New York: Whittlesey House, 1950), p. 148.

PP. 134–35, "THE NORTHEAST SECTION OF THE CITY"; "PRAIRIE GRASSES AND FLOWERS PUSH AGAINST THE DOORSTEPS": Federal Writers' Project, *Illinois*, pp. 303, 304.

P. 136, "NEGROES HAVE THEIR OWN SCHOOLS": ibid., p. 310.

P. 137, "VACANT LOTS ALONG SIDE STREETS": ibid.

PP. 137–38, "RESIDENTIAL ALTON LIES CHIEFLY . . . ON THE BLUFFS": ibid., p. 136.

P. 138, "THIS WORKMAN SPENDS THE MAJOR PORTION OF HIS TIME": Quincy Chamber of Commerce, *Quincy, Illinois, in the Heart of the Great Valley* (Quincy: Jost & Kiefer Printing Co., 1924), n.p.

P. 144, "SWEDES AND CALVINISM PREVAILED": Masters, *Sangamon*, p. 220.

P. 145, "IDEALISM, OPTIMISM, MATERIALISM": Lewis Atherton, *Main Street on the Middle Border* (Bloomington: Indiana University Press, 1954), p. xvi.

P. 145, "THE COUNTRY TOWN IS ONE OF THE GREAT AMERICAN INSTITUTIONS": Thorstein Veblen, "The Country Town," *The Freeman*, July 11, 1923, p. 418.

P. 145, "WALK INTO ANY DRUG OR BOOK STORE": Theodore Dreiser, *A Hoosier Holiday* (New York: John Lane, 1916), p. 448.

P. 146, "THE WORD LINGERS": Rose Wilder Lane, *Old Home Town* (New York: Longmans, Green, 1935), p. 2.

P. 147, "A COUNTY SEAT TOWN WAS TREMENDOUSLY IMPORTANT": Homer Croy, *Corn Country* (New York: Duell, Sloan & Pearce, 1947), p. 55.

P. 147, "THE BANK OR BANKS, A BATTERY OF LAWYERS' OFFICES": Hutton, *Midwest at Noon*, p. 79.

P. 147, ILLINOIS TOWN SIZES: Paul D. Converse, *Business Mortality of Illinois Retail Stores from 1925 to 1930* (Urbana: University of Illinois, 1932), p. 9.

P. 148, "ALL RIGHT, BOYS, GO AHEAD": Abraham Lincoln, quoted in Hansen, *Illinois*, p. 677.

P. 150, "MUCH OF THE SHAPE, LAYOUT, COMPACTNESS": Hutton, *Midwest at Noon*, p. 80.

P. 151, "THE PRAIRIE WAS INTERSECTED BY TWO RAILROADS": Mary Hartwell Catherwood, *The Spirit of an Illinois Town, and The Little Renault: Two Stories of Illinois, at Different Periods* (Boston: Houghton, Mifflin, 1897), p. 1.

P. 151, "RUNNING ALONGSIDE THE TRACK": John A. Kouwenhoven, *The Beer Can by the Highway: Essays on What's "American" about America* (Garden City, NY: Doubleday, 1961), p. 14.

PP. 152, 155, "THERE IS ALWAYS ONE LEADING HOTEL": Hutton, *Midwest at Noon*, p. 81.

P. 156, "THE SHRINE OF LEISURE AND TOLERANCE WAS NO MORE": Ferdinand Reyher, *I Heard Them Sing* (Boston: Little, Brown, 1946), p. 185.

P. 159, "MOST OF THE TOWNS YOU GO THROUGH ARE SMALL": Kouwenhoven, *Beer Can by the Highway*, p. 14.

P. 159, "TWO STORIED, WITH UNSHADED WINDOWS": Lane, *Old Home Town*, p. 3.

PP. 159–60, "ADDICTED TO 'THINGS' RATHER THAN IDEAS": Atherton, *Main Street on the Middle Border*, p. 250.

P. 161, "ACROSS THE FRONT OF THE HOUSE THERE WAS INVARIABLY A PORCH": Lane, *Old Home Town*, p. 7.

P. 161, "I GREW UP IN A MORNING-GLORY TOWN": Dave Etter, " "Porch Light," in *The Last Train to Prophetstown: Poems* (Lincoln: University of Nebraska Press, 1968), p. 19.

P. 161, "OWNERS WANTING A MEASURE OF INDIVIDUALITY": Atherton, *Main Street on the Middle Border*, p. 143.

P. 163, "THERE IT LAY IN THE MIND'S EYE": Carl Van Doren, "Sinclair Lewis and the Revolt from the Village," in *Twentieth Century Interpretations of Arrowsmith: A Collection of Critical Essays*, edited by Robert J. Griffen (Englewood Cliffs, NJ: Prentice-Hall, 1968), p. 83.

P. 166, "HE CONFINES HIS SERMONS": E. T. Hiller, Faye E. Corner, and Wendell L. East, *Rural Community Types* (Urbana: University of Illinois, 1928), p. 47.

P. 168, "IN THE EVENING EVERYONE TAKES DOWN THE RECEIVER": Vachel Lindsay, "An Editorial for the Wise Man in the Metropolis: Concerning the Humble Agricultural Village in Central Illinois," in Vachel Lindsay, *The Village Magazine* (1920), reprinted in *The Prose of Vachel Lindsay: Complete & with Lindsay's Drawings*, vol. 1, edited by Dennis Camp (Peoria: Spoon River Poetry Press, 1988), p. 128.

P. 168, "THESE FORCES ARE REPRESENTED": John A. Kinneman and Richard G. Browne, *America in Transition* (New York: McGraw-Hill, 1942), p. 115.

P. 168, RADIO STATION KYW: Rich Samuels, "It All Began with an Oath and an Opera: Behind the Scenes at Chicago's First Broadcast," http://www.richsamuels.com/nbcmm/kyw.html. (This online article is "a slightly modified version of an article written by the curator that appeared in the November 8th, 1993 edition of the 'Tempo' section of the *Chicago Tribune* on the occasion of the 62nd anniversary of Chicago's first broadcast.")

PP. 168–69, "THE HEIGHT OF THOSE ANTENNAS": Kouwenhoven, *Beer Can by the Highway*, p. 16.

P. 169, "A RESUME OF THE NATION'S ARCHITECTURAL EXPERIENCE": Federal Writers' Project, *Illinois*, pp. 333, 334.

PP. 169–71, "THE SLEEPY TOWN OF GALENA": Holiday, *American Panorama*, p. 193.

P. 172, "WAVING IN THE BREEZE OF EARLY MORNING": Federal Writers' Project, *Illinois*, p. 423.

P. 172, "THE FARMHOUSES AND FARM BUILDINGS OF THE MIDWEST": Hutton, *Midwest at Noon*, p. 70.

P. 172, "PROSPERITY, TRANQUILLITY, AND HAPPINESS": Lyell D. Henry, Jr., *Was This Heaven? A Self-Portrait of Iowa on Early Postcards* (Iowa City: University of Iowa Press, 1995), p. 50.

P. 173, "THE SEVERE SELF-RELIANCE IN THE FARMER'S STRUGGLE": Hutton, *Midwest at Noon*, p. 85.

P. 173, "THEIR ATTITUDE HAS ALWAYS BEEN THAT OF THE DEBTOR": ibid., p. 89.

P. 174, "NEITHER COULD HE CLOSE DOWN THE FARM": Edmund de S. Brunner, Gwendolyn S. Hughes, and Marjorie Patten, *American Agricultural Villages* (New York: George H. Doran, 1927), p. 44.

P. 174, "A ROUTINE AND PATTERN OF LIFE": Hutton, *Midwest at Noon*, p. 88.

P. 175, "PULL OFF THE HIGHWAY ON A WARM, HUMID NIGHT": Holiday, *American Panorama*, p. 188.

P. 176, "TO CONTEMPLATE THE PRAIRIES": Masters, *Sangamon*, p. 25.

P. 176, "THE PRAIRIE HAS BECOME, IN FACT, A TECHNOLOGICAL LANDSCAPE": Kouwenhoven, *Beer Can by the Highway*, p. 16.

P. 176, "UNAPPRECIATED BEAUTY OF PLAINNESS": Peattie, "The Best State of the Fifty."

P. 178, "BUT IN SOUTHERN ILLINOIS RAIN FELL": Baker Brownell, *The Other Illinois* (New York: Duell, Sloan & Pearce, 1958), p. 5.

P. 178, "MAGNOLIAS, SOUTHERN PINE, AND NORTHERN OAK": John H. Keiser, *Building for the Centuries: Illinois, 1865 to 1898* (Urbana: University of Illinois Press, 1977), p. 4.

P. 179, "ASTIR WITH GROWERS OF CORN, COTTON, AND APPLES": Federal Writers' Project, *Illinois*, p. 171.

P. 180, "50 POINTS OF INTEREST": Hansen, *Illinois*, p. 640.

P. 182, "ARCADIA": Peter J. Schmitt, *Back to Nature: The Arcadian Myth in Urban America* (New York: Oxford University Press, 1969), p. xvii.

Credits

Figure 41. E. C. Kropp Co. (#906), Milwaukee.

Figure 42. Hotel Sherman, Chicago.

Figure 43. Hotel La Salle, Chicago.

Figure 44. Hilton Litho. Co., Chicago.

Figure 45. A. C. Co. (#227).

Figure 46. American Colortype (#307), Chicago and New York.

Figure 47. United States Post Card and Novelty Co. (#88), Chicago.

Figure 48. V. O. Hammon Pub. Co. (#7319), Chicago.

Figure 49. Franklin Post Card Co. (#458).

Figure 50. Kunz Brothers Specialty Co. (#108706), Chicago.

Figure 51. Gerson Brothers (#112), Chicago.

Figure 52a. A. C. Co. (#209).

Figure 52b. Max Rigot Selling Co. (Century of Progress issue #200), Chicago.

Figure 53. No publisher given; printed in Germany (#110).

Figure 54. No publisher given; printed in Germany (#189).

Figure 55a. P. Schmidt & Co. (#867), Chicago; made in Germany.

Figure 55b. V. O. Hammon Pub. Co. (#703), Chicago.

Figure 56. A. C. Co. (#3268).

Figure 57. Max Rigot Selling Agency (#282), Chicago; American Colortype, Chicago.

*Figure 58a. Curt Teich & Co., Chicago.

Figure 58b. Armour & Co. (Reg. No. 360316), Chicago.

Figure 59. V. O. Hammon Pub. Co. (#1958), Chicago.

Figure 60. Max Rigot Selling Agency (#209), Chicago; Colortype, Chicago.

Figure 61. V. O. Hammon Pub. Co. (#1953), Chicago.

Figure 62. Illinois Central Railroad (#4044), Chicago.

Figure 63. College Inn Products.

Figure 64. [Union News Co.] (#58478).

Figure 65. No publisher given.

Figure 66. Sears, Roebuck & Co. (#F7632), Chicago.

Figure 67. V. O. Hammon Pub. Co. (#700), Chicago.

Figure 68. Acmegraph Co. (#108c), Chicago.

Figure 69. Acmegraph Co. (#180c), Chicago.

Figure 70. Snapshot photo, privately printed on post-card paper.

Figure 71. Snapshot photo, privately printed on post-card paper.

Figure 72. Snapshot photo, privately printed on post-card paper.

Figure 73. Snapshot photo, privately printed on post-card paper.

Figure 74. Snapshot photo, privately printed on post-card paper.

Figure 75. Snapshot photo, privately printed on post-card paper.

Figure 76. Snapshot photo, privately printed on post-card paper.

Figure 77. V. O. Hammon Pub. Co. (#1878), Chicago.

Figure 78. Alfred Holzmann (#202291), Chicago.

Figure 79. Franklin Post Card Co. (#454), Chicago.

Figure 80. V. O. Hammon Pub. Co. (#1335), Chicago.

Figure 81. Max Rigot Selling Co., Chicago (#272); C. T. American Art.

Figure 82. Snapshot photo, privately printed on post-card paper.

Figure 83. No publisher given.

Figure 84. Max Rigot (#R-50378), Chicago.

Figure 85. S. H. Knox & Co., Chicago; printed in Germany.

Figure 86. White City Construction Co., Chicago.

Figure 87a. Max Rigot Selling Agency (#251), Chicago; American Colortype, Chicago and New York.

Figure 87b. Museum of Science and Industry, Chicago; Plastichrome, Colorpicture, Boston.

Figure 88. A Century of Progress, Chicago's 1933 International Exposition, Chicago (#113).

*Figure 89. Curt Teich & Co. (#162), Chicago; C. T. Art-Colortone.

Figure 90. Alfred Holzmann, Publisher, Chicago and Leipzig.

Figure 91. Hugh C. Leighton Co., Portland, Maine; printed in Frankfort-on-Main, Germany.

Figure 92. Raphael Tuck (#2206), London.

Figure 93. Charles R. Childs, Chicago.

Figure 94. Remien and Kuhnert Co., Chicago.

Figure 95. E. C. Kropp Co., Milwaukee.

Figure 96. Max Rigot Selling Agency, Chicago; American Colortype Co., Chicago.

*Figure 97. Curt Teich & Co., Chicago; C. T. Art-Colortone.

Figure 98. Groghan Photo Service, Chicago.

Figure 99. L. L. Cook Co., Milwaukee.

Figure 100. C. T. American Art Colored, Chicago.

Figure 101a. Raphael Tuck (#2206), London.

Figure 101b. N. J. (#583), Buffalo, N.Y.; printed in Germany.

Figure 102. C. R. Childs (#3201), Chicago; Brooks Photo.

*Figure 103. Curt Teich & Co. (#345), Chicago.

Figure 104. Acmegraph (#6184), Chicago.

Figure 105a. S. H. Knox & Co., Chicago; printed in Germany.

Figure 105b. V. O. Hammon Pub. Co., Chicago.

*Figure 106. Curt Teich & Co. (#176-30), Chicago; C. T. American Art; Harry G. Beach, photographer.

Figure 107. V. O. Hammon Pub. Co. (#283), Chicago.

Figure 108. United Airlines, Chicago; Kodachrome by E. D. McGlone.

Figure 109. Fred Harvey Co. (#9C-K762), Chicago.

Figure 110. Dexter Color Illinois, Inc. (#8063-C), Chicago.

*Figure 111. Curt Teich & Co. (#8A-H1342), Chicago; Art-Colortone.

Figure 112. A. J. Ironmonger's City Drug Store, publisher (#671); made in Germany.

Figure 113. No publisher given (#606).

Figure 114. Raphael Tuck (Lincoln's Birthday series, #155).

Figure 115. U.S. Postal Card; Geo Coldewey, Publisher (#9129), Springfield, Ill.

*Figure 116. Curt Teich & Co. (#1A-H157), Chicago; C. T. Art-Colortone; H. N. Shonkwiler, Springfield, Ill.

Figure 117. Sears, Roebuck & Co., Chicago.

*Figure 118. Curt Teich & Co. (#96062-N), Chicago; C. T. American Art; Peoria Candy Co.

*Figure 119. Curt Teich & Co. (#6A-H835), Chicago; C. T. PhotoColorit.

Figure 120. Souvenir Post Card Station (#6822), Davenport, Iowa.

Figure 121a. Rock Island Post Card Co. (#53), Rock Island, Ill.

Figure 121b. Rock Island Post Card Co. (#578), Rock Island, Ill.

Figure 122. E. C. Kropp (#20271-N), Milwaukee.

Figure 123. Color-View, Inc. (#6275-C), Rockford, Ill.; photo by H. Bruechner; printed by Dexter Press, West Nyack, N.Y.

Figure 124. No publisher given; printed in Germany.

Figure 125. Spafford & Co. Photographers, Bloomington, Ill.

Figure 126. Read and White, Publishers (#4006), Bloomington, Ill.

Figure 127. W. B. Read & Co. (#4016), Bloomington, Ill.; C. T. Photocrom.

Figure 128. Lloyd's [Drug Store].

Figure 129. Snapshot photo, privately printed on postcard paper.

Figure 130. Strauch's Student Life Series, Champaign, Ill.

Figure 131. Gerson Brothers (#14779), Chicago.

Figure 132. E. C. Kropp, Milwaukee.

*Figure 133. Curt Teich & Co. (#2B-H130), Chicago; C. T. Art-Colortone; Decatur News Agency, Decatur, Ill.

*Figure 134. Curt Teich & Co., Chicago; C. T. American Art; Decatur News Agency, Decatur, Ill.

Figure 135. St. Louis News Co. (#43347), St. Louis.

*Figure 136. C. T. [Curt Teich] Photochrom (#A-4057).

Figure 137. Acmegraph Co. (#10096), Chicago.

*Figure 138. Curt Teich & Co., Chicago.

Figure 139. C. E. Wetzel (#76-49), Quincy, Ill.

Figure 140. B. & C. Distributing Co., Haysville, Kans.; lithograph by Henry McGrew Printing Co., Kansas City, Mo.

*Figure 141. C. T. [Curt Teich] American Art (#A-92316), Chicago.

* Figure 142. C. T. [Curt Teich] American Art (#R-20740).

*Figure 143a. Curt Teich & Co. (#103895), Chicago.

Figure 143b. No publisher given.

Figure 144. Schimmel Hotels, Inc., Omaha.

Figure 145. A. H.; printed in Germany.

Figure 146. L. E. Janzen, Bunker Hill, Ill.; printed in Germany.

Figure 147. E. C. Kropp Co. (Monmouth, Ill., #10), Milwaukee.

*Figure 148. Curt Teich & Co., Chicago; C. T. American Art.

Figure 149. A. O. Elliott (#U.S. 502), Savanna, Ill.

Figure 150. No publisher given.

Figure 151. J. S. Baker, San Jose, Ill.

Figure 152a. H. H. Bregstone, St. Louis.

Figure 152b. Benke, Salem, Ill.

*Figure 153. Curt Teich & Co. (#123922), Chicago.

*Figure 154. Curt Teich & Co. (#99266), Chicago.

Figure 155. P. L. Huckins, Chicago.

Figure 156. L. L. Cook (#L0817), Milwaukee.

Figure 157. No publisher given.

Figure 158. C. U. Williams, Bloomington, Ill.

Figure 159. No publisher given.

Figure 160a. No publisher given.

Figure 160b. ONY (#PC6).

Figure 161. Post Office News Stand (#107), Geneseo, Ill.; made in Germany.

Figure 162. M. C. Hood (#C8855), Havana, Ill.; Litho-Chrome, Leipzig, Berlin, and Dresden, Germany.

Figure 163. Snapshot photo, privately printed on post-card paper.

Figure 164. No publisher given.

Figure 165. No publisher given.

Figure 166. No publisher given.

Figure 167. No publisher given.

Figure 168. E. C. Kropp Co. (#12446N), Milwaukee.

Figure 169. American Telephone & Telegraph Co., New York.

Figure 170. E. C. Kropp Co. (Harrisburg #12), Milwaukee.

Figure 171. Wait's Green Mountain Cough Syrup.

Figure 172. No publisher given.

Figure 173. Color-View Inc. (#63769-B), Rockford, Ill.; Ektachrome by Joe E. Clark; Dexter Press, West Nyack, N.Y.

*Figure 174. Curt Teich & Co., Chicago; C. T. American Art.

Figure 175. Snapshot photo, privately printed on post-card paper.

Figure 176. Snapshot photo, privately printed on post-card paper.

Figure 177. Snapshot photo, privately printed on post-card paper.

Figure 178. Snapshot photo, privately printed on post-card paper.

Figure 179. H. W. Buckbee Co., Rockford, Ill.

Figure 180a. Witt (#2012).

Figure 180b. Talbott Eno Co., Des Moines, Iowa.

Figure 181. Hamilton Photo Co., Ames, Iowa.

*Figure 182. Curt Teich & Co., Chicago; C. T. American Art; Cairo News Co., Cairo, Ill.

Figure 183. International Post Card Co. (#550), New York; made in Germany.

Figure 184. Snapshot photo, privately printed on post-card paper.

Figure 185. Kneussl Brothers (#602), Ottawa, Ill.

Figure 186. B. Sebastian (#171), Chicago.

Figure 187. No publisher given.

Note: The asterisk, *, designates postcards courtesy of Lake County [Ill.] Museum, Curt Teich Archives. The Curt Teich Postcard Archives at the Lake County Museum near Wauconda, Illinois, is the largest public collection of postcards in the United States. There one will find files detailing some 100,000 postcards published by Chicago's Curt Teich and Company between 1898 and 1978. The collection includes some 365,000 postcards. The archive also contains postcards published by V. O. Hammon and the Detroit Publishing Company. The Abraham Lincoln Library in Springfield, Illinois, holds some 5,200 postcards related to Abraham Lincoln and the state of Illinois.

Index

JOHN A. JAKLE is a professor
emeritus of geography at the University
of Illinois at Urbana-Champaign.

KEITH A. SCULLE is the former
head of research and education for the Illinois
Historic Preservation Agency.

Together they have coauthored several books,
including *Fast Food: Roadside Restaurants in
the Automobile Age, The Motel in America,*
and *The Gas Station in America.*

The University of Illinois Press
is a founding member of the
Association of American University Presses.

———————————————————————

Designed by Kelly Gray
Composed in 9.5/14 The Serif Semi Light
with Scala Sans display
by Jim Proefrock
at the University of Illinois Press
Manufactured by Sheridan Books, Inc.

University of Illinois Press
1325 South Oak Street
Champaign, IL 61820-6903
www.press.uillinois.edu